HEE!
HA!
HA!
CHUCKLE!
YUK! YUK!
HO!
HA!
HA-HA!
HA!
GUFFAW!
HEE-HEE!
HA!

HYUK!

THE MIGHTY BIG BOOK OF SCHOOL JOKES

HO!

LIBRARY O' LAUGHS

ALL MY LOVE 2

AVARELLE

-DAD

 PUBLISHED BY PRICE STERN SLOAN, A DIVISION OF PENGUIN YOUNG READERS GROUP, 345 HUDSON STREET, NEW YORK, NY 10014. MANUFACTURED IN CHINA.

LIBRARY OF CONGRESS CONTROL NUMBER: 2003103418

ISBN 978-0-8431-7790-9 10 9 8 7 6 5 4 3 2 1

SPECIAL MARKETS ISBN 978-0-8431-7305-5

THE MIGHTY BIG BOOK™ OF SCHOOL JOKES

HO!

by Craig Yoe

LIBRARY O' LAUGHS

PSS!
PRICE STERN SLOAN
An Imprint of Penguin Group (USA) Inc.

THANKS TO MY ***"CLASSY CLASSMATES":***
JON ANDERSON, KELLI CHIPPONERI, ANNMARIE HARRIS, CLIZIA GUSSONI, JAYNE ANTIPOW, ADAM GARBER, REBECCA GOLDBERG, AND ***PATRICIA PASQUALE.***

MAD ADD JOKE!

AQUARIUM
+ SHEEP
TANK EWE

SCHOOL IS ALL ABOUT THE ***"4 R'S":*** ***READING, 'RITING, 'RITHMETIC,*** AND ***RIDDLES!*** AND THIS ***BOOK*** HAS THEM ***ALL:*** I ***WROTE*** IT, YOU'RE ***READING*** IT, AND THERE'S ABOUT ***8 GAZILLION RIDDLES*** IN IT (286 PAGES ***X*** 4 RIDDLES ON A PAGE = 8 GAZILLION...OKAY, SO MAYBE MY ***'RITHMETIC*** ISN'T SO GOOD).

ANYHOO, YOU KNOW HOW YOU HAVE ***BOOKS*** THAT HELP YOU ***LEARN*** ABOUT ***HISTORY, SCIENCE,*** AND ***STUFF*** LIKE THAT? WELL, CONSIDER ***THIS*** THE BOOK THAT WILL HELP YOU LEARN HOW TO ***LAUGH!*** BEST OF ALL, WITH THIS BOOK THERE'S ***NO HOMEWORK!*** BUT THERE ***WILL*** BE A ***TEST***...SO TURN THE PAGE AND ***START STUDYING!***

YOUR PAL,
CRAIG YOE.

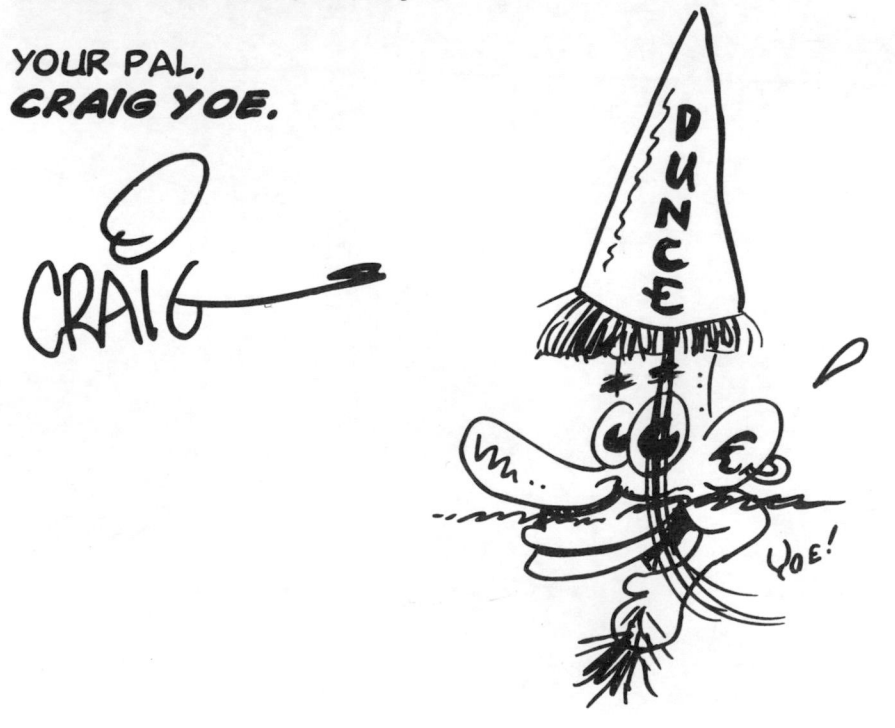

CRAIG

WHY DID THE ***DOG*** DO
SO ***WELL*** IN ***SCHOOL?***

... BECAUSE HE WAS THE ***TEACHER'S PET!***

WHICH ***SCHOOL SUBJECT*** DO
RUNNERS LIKE MOST?

... GE-***JOG***-RAPHY!

POETRY CLASS

WHAT DO YOU CALL AN OLD,
DECAYING TABLE?

A grotesque desk!

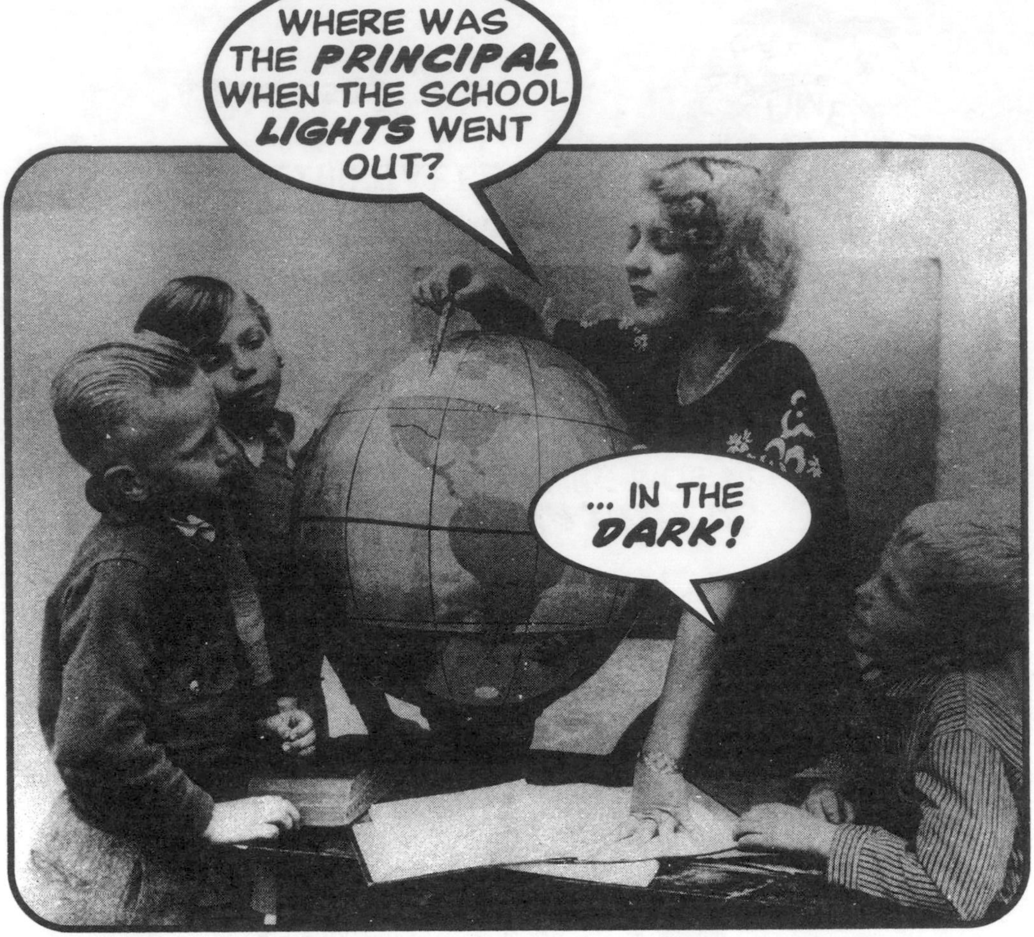

WHAT DID THE **STUDENTS** SEE ON THE **DESK** IN **WOOD SHOP?**

... THEY **SAW DUST!**

MAD® ADD JOKE!

BUBBLE GUM
\+ LOCOMOTIVE
CHEW-CHEW TRAIN

LUNCH LADY
YOE!

WHAT IS A LUNCH LADY'S FAVORITE SCHOOL SUBJECT?

... *Spam-ish!*

WHO **FIRST** USED **FRACTIONS?**
... LOUIS THE 1/16!

WHICH IS THE ***FRIENDLIEST*** SCHOOL?

... ***HI*** SCHOOL!

WHAT DID THE ***ASTRONAUT'S MOTHER*** GIVE HIM ON THE WAY TO SCHOOL?

... ***LAUNCH*** MONEY!

FRED: WOULD YOU ***LIKE*** TO HEAR HOW I LEARNED TO **TIE** MY **SHOES** IN KINDERGARTEN?

NED: I'D RATHER ***KNOT!***

ENGLISH TEACHER: WHAT IS THE ***DIFFERENCE*** BETWEEN ***HERE*** AND ***THERE?***

SMART ALECK: THE LETTER ***"T"!***

WHAT DO YOU CALL ***SOMEONE*** WHO WEARS A ***UNIFORM,*** CARRIES ***POM-POMS,*** AND LIVES IN THE ***FOREST?***

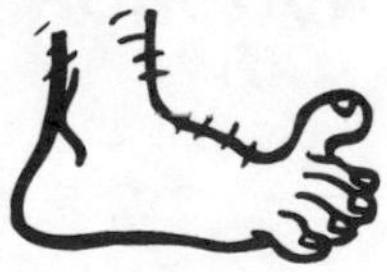

... A ***DEER***-LEADER!

WHERE DOES A ***FISHERMAN*** WRITE HIS ***HOMEWORK ASSIGNMENTS?***

... IN A ***NET***-BOOK!

WHICH ***INSECT*** GETS THE ***BEST GRADES*** IN ***ENGLISH?***

... THE ***BOOKWORM!***

MUSIC TEACHER: HOW CAN I ***FIX*** THIS ***BROKEN HORN?***

SCHOOL CUSTODIAN: WITH A ***TUBA*** GLUE!

WHAT DID THE ***ART TEACHER*** SAY WHEN THE ***STUDENTS*** ASKED HER IF ***PAINTING*** IS ***DIFFICULT?***

... "NO, IT'S ***EASEL!***"

WHY DID THE ***CHICKEN*** CROSS THE ***PLAYGROUND?***

... TO GET TO THE OTHER ***SLIDE!***

WHY DID THE SHEEP GO TO THE SCHOOL NURSE?

... She wasn't feeling wool!

WHY DID THE DUCK GET SENT TO THE PRINCIPAL'S OFFICE?
... HE WAS A WISE-QUACKER!
WHAT IS TARZAN'S FAVORITE THING TO PLAY ON IN THE SCHOOLYARD?
... THE JUNGLE GYM!
WHAT WORD IS ALWAYS SPELLED RIGHT?
... RIGHT!

WHAT DO YOU ***SAY*** TO SOMEONE WHO JUST ***FINISHED*** HIGH SCHOOL?

... "CON-***GRAD***-ULATIONS!"

WHICH ***COLOR*** SHOULD A ***CHEERLEADER'S*** UNIFORM BE?

... ***YELL***-OW!

WHY DID THE ***SCHOOL BASKETBALL COACH*** MAKE HIS PLAYERS ***WEAR BIBS?***

... BECAUSE THEY WERE ***ALWAYS DRIBBLING!***

WHICH TYPE OF CANDY DO YOU EAT IN THE SCHOOLYARD?
... RECESS PIECES!
CRAYON

WHICH **SCHOOL** HAS THE BEST **KARATE** TEAM?

... **HI-YA** SCHOOL!

BASKETBALL PLAYER: **COACH,** I WENT TO THE **DOCTOR** AND HE SAID **I CAN'T PLAY BASKETBALL!**

COACH: YOU DIDN'T NEED A **DOCTOR** TO TELL YOU **THAT!**

SUE: WHY ARE YOU ***WRITING*** WITH A ***CARROT?***

STU: OH NO! I MUST HAVE ***EATEN*** MY ***PENCIL!***

MAD® ADD JOKE!

MARMALADE
+ TROUT

JELLY FISH

WHAT'S THE MOST ***DANGEROUS*** THING TO ***ORDER*** IN THE ***SCHOOL CAFETERIA?***

... PIRANHA-INFESTED TOMATO SOUP!

MARY: I HEAR THE ***SCHOOL PLAY*** HAS A ***HAPPY ENDING!***

GARY: YEAH, EVERYONE WAS ***HAPPY*** WHEN IT ***ENDED!***

WHAT DO ***VAMPIRES*** EAT IN THE ***CAFETERIA?***

... ***FANG***-FURTERS!

HOW DO YOU KNOW A ***DINOSAUR*** IS IN YOUR ***LOCKER?***

... YOU CAN'T ***SHUT*** THE ***DOOR!***

COUNSELOR CRACK UPS!

WHY DID THE MATH TEST GO TO SEE THE SCHOOL COUNSELOR?

Because it had lots of problems!

WHY WAS THE ***BELLY BUTTON POPULAR*** IN SCHOOL?

... IT WAS PART OF THE ***INNIE CROWD!***

HOW DOES THE PRINCIPAL GET TO SCHOOL?
... ON THE SCHOOL BOSS!

WHICH ***SCHOOL BAND MUSICAL INSTRUMENT*** CAN YOU USE TO CATCH ***FISH?***

... A CLARI-***NET!***

WHY DID THE **GOLFER** DO SO **WELL** IN **SCHOOL?**

... HE WAS THE **TEACHER'S PUTT!**

WHAT DID THE **STRAIGHT-A STUDENT** ORDER IN THE **SCHOOL CAFETERIA?**

... AN **HONOR ROLL!**

WHICH KIND OF ***SANDWICHES*** DO ***TEMPORARY TEACHERS*** EAT?

... ***SUBS!***

WHAT IS THE SCHOOL ***BAND'S*** FAVORITE ***MONTH?***

... ***MARCH!***

POETRY CLASS

WHAT DO YOU CALL IT WHEN YOU GET AN A+ ON AN EXAM?

Your best test!

GEOGRAPHY TEACHER: WHAT IS IN THE **CENTER** OF BOTH **GEORGIA** AND **FLORIDA?**

SMART ALECK: THE **LETTER "R"!**

LETTER LAFFS

WHICH LETTER IS HARD OF HEARING?

A!

TOM: I AIN'T GOT NO PAPER!
TEACHER: I HAVEN'T ANY PAPER!
TOM: YOU AND ME BOTH!
WHAT DO YOU SAY TO THE SCHOOL LIBRARIAN WHEN YOU LEAVE YOUR BOOKS OUTSIDE OVERNIGHT?
"SORRY, MY BOOKS ARE OVER-DEW!"
TEACHER: WHAT DID SIR ISAAC NEWTON SAY WHEN HE DISCOVERED GRAVITY?
TOM: "OUCH!"

TEACHER: IF YOU HAVE ***THREE*** PIECES OF CANDY AND YOUR ***MOTHER*** ASKS YOU TO GIVE YOUR SISTER ***ONE,*** HOW MANY PIECES WILL YOU HAVE ***LEFT?***

TOM: THREE!

WHY WAS THE ***INSECT*** EXCITED WHEN HE SAW HIS ***REPORT CARD?***

... BECAUSE HE GOT ***KILLER BEES!***

WHICH ***SCHOOL*** HAS THE BEST ***FOOTBALL TEAM?***

... ***HIKE*** SCHOOL!

WHAT DOES A ***FOOT EAT*** WHEN THE CAFETERIA SERVES ***MEXICAN FOOD?***
... BURRI-***TOES!***
YOE!

MAD ADD JOKE!

PIG
+ MARTIAL ARTS

PORK CHOPS!

WHAT DOES AN ASTRONOMER GET ON HIS PAPER WHEN HE DOES WELL?
... GOLD STARS!
WHAT DID THE MONKEY GET ON HIS FINALS?
... ALL APES!
LUNCH LADY
YOE!
WHAT DID THE LUNCH LADY SERVE THE GYM COACH?
... Soccer-tash!

WHAT IS THE ***PHYSICAL EDUCATION*** TEACHER'S ***NAME?***

... ***JIM NASIUM!***

WHAT KIND OF ***CEREAL*** DOES A ***MATH TEACHER*** EAT?

... AN ALGE-***BRAN!***

WHAT DOES A GHOST EAT WHEN THE SCHOOL CAFETERIA SERVES ITALIAN FOOD?
... SPOOK-GHETTI!

HOW DO ***DONKEYS*** GET TO ***SCHOOL*** EVERY DAY?

... THE ***MULE*** BUS!

WHY ARE ***CALCULATORS*** SO ***RELIABLE?***

... BECAUSE YOU CAN ***COUNT*** ON THEM!

WHICH KIND OF ***TREE*** IS ***GOOD AT MATH?***

... A ***GEOME-TREE!***

MOM: WHAT'S THE MEANING OF THIS "***F***" ON YOUR ***REPORT CARD?***

TOM: "*FABULOUS!*"

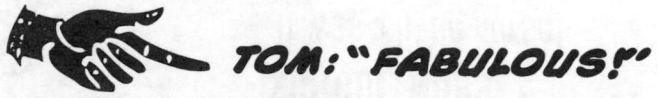

WHY SHOULDN'T YOU DO YOUR ***HOMEWORK*** ON AN ***EMPTY STOMACH?***

... IT'S BETTER TO USE ***PAPER!***

WHICH LETTER STINGS?

B!

TEACHER: HOW MANY **STATES** ARE THERE IN THE **UNITED STATES?**

TOM: I DON'T **KNOW.**

TEACHER: YOU'RE IN THE **FIFTH GRADE** AND YOU **DON'T KNOW** HOW MANY **STATES** THERE ARE?

TOM: WELL, **YOU'RE** THE **TEACHER** AND **YOU** DON'T KNOW!

ADAM: WHEN I **GROW UP** I WANT TO JOIN THE **CIRCUS!**

SCHOOL COUNSELOR: STOP **CLOWNING AROUND!**

School Nurse Sick Jokes

WHY DID THE PONY GO TO THE SCHOOL NURSE?

... It was a little horse!

TEACHER: ARE YOU TAKING A ***NAP*** BACK THERE?

MIKE: HOW ***CAN*** I IF YOU ***KEEP TALKING?***

WHEN THE ***RUNNER*** CAME IN ***SECOND PLACE,*** WHAT DID THE ***COACH*** TELL HIM TO ***EAT?***

... KETCHUP!

TRACEY: IS IT ***LUNCHTIME?***

TEACHER: NOT FOR ANOTHER ***30 MINUTES.***

TRACEY: OH, THEN MY ***STOMACH*** MUST BE ***FAST!***

GEOMETRY TEACHER: WHICH FIGURE IS LIKE A RUNAWAY PARROT?

TOM: A POLYGON!

WHAT DO YOU PUT AT THE END OF THE FIRST SENTENCE IN AN ESSAY?

... FIRST PERIOD!

WHAT SHOULD YOU DO WHEN YOUR TONGUE IS ALL RED?

... BRING IT BACK TO THE LIBRARY!

COUNSELOR CRACK UPS!

WHY DID THE LEAD IN THE SCHOOL PLAY GO TO THE SCHOOL COUNSELOR?

He wasn't himself today!

WHY DID THE ***GHOUL*** GET ***SAD*** ON HIS ***FIRST DAY AT SCHOOL?***

... HE MISSED HIS ***MUMMY!***

WHAT DO YOU CALL ***SOMEONE*** WHO WEARS A ***UNIFORM,*** CARRIES ***POM-POMS,*** AND IS ***ALWAYS SCARED?***

... A ***FEAR***-LEADER!

WHERE DO YOU ***GO*** AFTER EATING ***BEANS*** IN THE ***SCHOOL CAFETERIA?***

... ***FART CLASS!***

WHICH ***TEAM*** DO ***KIDS WITH COLDS*** PLAY ON?

... THE ***SICKER*** TEAM!

MAD® ADD JOKE!

COW SPEAK
\+ JEWELRY
MOOO-D RING

SCHOOL TEAM HOMERUN HA-HA'S

WHICH ***POSITION*** WOULD A ***DOG*** PLAY ON THE SCHOOL ***BASEBALL*** TEAM?

... ***POOCHER!***

WHICH ***POSITION*** WOULD A ***DRY CLEANER*** PLAY ON THE SCHOOL ***BASEBALL*** TEAM?

... ***SHIRT***-STOP!

WHICH ***POSITION*** WOULD A ***FISHERMAN*** PLAY ON THE SCHOOL ***BASEBALL*** TEAM?

... ***CATCHER!***

WHICH ***POSITION*** WOULD AN ***ELEVATOR*** PLAY ON THE SCHOOL ***BASEBALL*** TEAM?

... ***LIFT*** FIELD!

WHICH ***POSITION*** WOULD AN ***ORANGE*** PLAY ON THE SCHOOL ***BASEBALL*** TEAM?

... ***RIPE*** FIELD!

GYM TEACHER: CAN YOU **STAND** ON YOUR **HEAD?**

SMART ALECK: NO, IT'S **TOO HIGH UP!**

HOW DO YOU KNOW THE ENGLISH TEACHER'S SNAKE IS A BABY?
... IT HAS A RATTLE!

KNOCK-KNOCK?
... WHO'S THERE?
JEWEL!
... JEWEL WHO?
JEWEL DO YOUR **HOMEWORK** IF YOU KNOW WHAT'S **GOOD FOR YOU!**

TEACHER: USE THE WORD **"UNAWARE"** IN A **SENTENCE.**

CLIZIA: I WAS IN A **HURRY** TODAY SO I DIDN'T **WEAR** ANY **UNAWARE!**

School Nurse Sick Jokes

Dan: I don't like this pimple on my nose!

School Nurse: It'll grow on you!

TEACHER: WHO CAN TELL ME ***WHERE*** THE ***DECLARATION OF INDEPENDENCE*** WAS SIGNED?

TOM: AT THE ***BOTTOM!***

WHAT IS A ***SONGWRITER'S*** FAVORITE THING TO ***PLAY ON*** IN THE ***SCHOOLYARD?***

... THE ***JINGLE*** GYM!

WHY DID THE ***CHARGE CARD*** TURN IN MORE ***HOMEWORK?***

... IT WANTED EXTRA ***CREDIT!***

ENGLISH TEACHER: HOW DO YOU MAKE A ***HAT TALK?***

SMART ALECK: PUT A ***"C" IN FRONT OF IT!***

COUNSELOR CRACK UPS!

WAYNE: WHEN I GROW UP I WANT TO BE A DRUMMER!

School Counselor: Beat it, kid!

WHAT DID THE ***GYM TEACHER*** MAKE THE ***CLASS CLOWN*** DO WHEN HE ACTED UP?
... ***JUMPING JOKES!***

WHERE DID THE ***SUPERHERO*** GO DURING ***SCHOOL VACATION?***

... ***CAPE*** COD!

DRAMA TEACHER: SOMEONE ***STOLE*** THE ***WIGS*** FOR THE ***SCHOOL PLAY!***

PRINCIPAL: WE'LL ***COMB*** THE SCHOOL FOR CLUES!

TEACHER: GARY, HAVE YOU ***FINISHED*** YOUR LIST OF THE ***NINE GREATEST AMERICANS?***

GARY: NOT YET. I CAN'T THINK OF A ***RIGHT FIELDER!***

WHICH KIND OF PIZZA DO DOGS ORDER IN THE SCHOOL CAFETERIA?
... PUP-PERONI!

WHAT DOES A ***BLACK, ORANGE, AND WHITE CAT*** USE IN ***MATH CLASS?***

... A ***CALICO***-LATOR!

WHAT ***TIME*** DO YOU HAVE TO GET OUT OF CLASS TO GO TO THE ***DENTIST?***

... ***TOOTH-HURTY!***

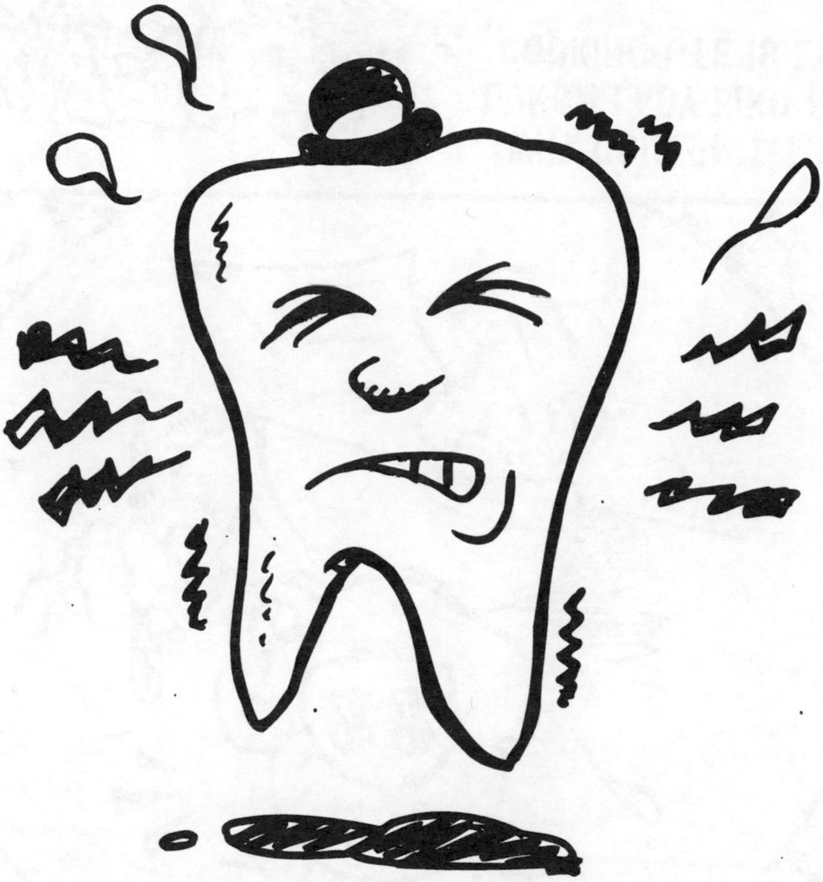

WHAT KIND OF ***TRANSPORTATION*** DO YOU USE TO GET TO THE ***BATHROOM?***

... THE ***TUB***-WAY!

WHICH LETTER CAN YOU SAIL ON?

C!

WHAT IS A COW'S FAVORITE CLASS?
... MOO-SIC
WHAT DOES A PIG USE TO TAKE NOTES?
... A PIG PEN!
YOE!
LUNCH LADY
YOE!
WHY COULDN'T THE LUNCH LADY FIND HER COOKING UTENSILS?
... The cat had her tong!

WHAT IS THE ***QUIETEST SCHOOL TEAM*** YOU CAN JOIN?

... THE ***BOWLING TEAM*** -- YOU CAN HEAR A ***PIN*** DROP!

WHY WAS THE PIG THROWN OUT OF THE SCHOOL FOOTBALL GAME?
... HE PLAYED DIRTY!

MOM: ARE YOU DOING YOUR ***GEOGRAPHY HOMEWORK?***

BILLY: YEP. WHERE IS THE ***EQUATOR?***

MOM: WHEREVER YOU LEFT IT! NOW FINISH THAT HOMEWORK ... ***NO EXCUSES!***

WHAT DOES A ***DOG*** ORDER IN THE ***SCHOOL CAFETERIA?***

... CHICKEN ***POODLE*** SOUP!

KNOCK, KNOCK!
... WHO'S THERE?
BESS!
... BESS WHO?
BESS PERSONALITY!

WHICH ***CAFETERIA FOOD*** MAKES YOU ***THROW UP?***

... ***SPEW***-GHETTI!

FIRST TEACHER: DO YOUR ***PUPILS*** ALWAYS ***SNORE*** IN ***CLASS?***

SECOND TEACHER: NO, ONLY ***WHEN*** THEY'RE ***SLEEPING!***

HOW DID THE ***CHICKEN WAKE UP*** FOR ***SCHOOL?***

... IT USED AN ***ALARM CLUCK!***

MAD® ADD JOKE!

TRUTHFUL
+ MONKEY
———————
HONEST APE!

ENGLISH TEACHER: WHY IS THE ***LETTER A*** LIKE A ***FLOWER?***

SMART ALECK: BECAUSE A ***BEE*** COMES AFTER IT!

HOW DID THE ***RABBIT REACT*** WHEN HE ***FAILED*** HIS ***TEST?***

... HE GOT ***HOPPING*** MAD!

LETTER LAFFS

WHICH LETTER DO YOU SEE WITH?

I!

WHAT IS THE ***LIBRARIAN'S NAME?***

... RITA BOOK!

AMERICAN HISTORY TEACHER: WHY DOES THE ***STATUE OF LIBERTY*** STAND IN NEW YORK HARBOR?

SMART ALECK: SHE CAN'T ***SIT DOWN!***

MATH TEACHER: HOW DO YOU MAKE THE ***NUMBER SEVEN EVEN?***

SMART ALECK: TAKE ***AWAY*** THE ***"S"!***

WHAT DID THE ART TEACHER USE TO PAINT THE RIVER?
... WATER-COLORS!

WHY CAN'T YOU TAKE AN ***ELEPHANT* TO SCHOOL?**

... BECAUSE IT WON'T ***FIT*** IN YOUR ***BACKPACK!***

TOM: I GOT A ***100*** IN ***SCHOOL*** TODAY!

MOM: THAT'S ***GREAT!***

TOM: YEAH, I GOT A ***30*** IN ***MATH,*** A ***45*** IN ***SCIENCE,*** AND A ***25*** IN ***ENGLISH!***

WHY WAS THE ***BIRD***
ABSENT FROM
SCHOOL?

... HE WAS FEELING
UNDER THE FEATHER!

School Nurse
SICK JOKES

WHY DID THE FISH GO TO THE SCHOOL NURSE?

... It wasn't feeling whale!

WHAT DID THE ***ART TEACHER*** DO
WHEN HE WAS A ***BABY?***

... HE ***DREW***-LED!

TEACHER: HOW DO YOU SPELL ***"WASHINGTON"?***

PATRICIA: THE ***STATE*** OR THE ***PRESIDENT?***

WHAT DID THE ***SCHOOL JANITOR*** GET WHEN HE WENT TO THE ***HOTEL?***

... ***BROOM*** SERVICE!

WHY DID THE LUNCH LADY COOK WITH SO MANY ONIONS?

... She found them ap-peel-ing!

CRAIG: I WANT TO ***SING SOLO*** IN THE ***GLEE CLUB!***

CLIZIA: OKAY. SING ***SO LOW*** WE ***CAN'T HEAR YOU!***

GEOGRAPHY TEACHER: WHICH ***CITY*** HAS ***TWO*** OF ***EVERYTHING?***

SMART ALECK: PAIR-IS!

WHAT DO **VULTURES EAT AFTER SCHOOL?**

... AN AFTER-SCHOOL **SNAKE!**

WHERE DOES A BARBER LEARN TO SHAVE CUSTOMERS?
... AT THE SCHOOL OF HARD NICKS!

SCIENCE TEACHER: WHAT IS THE **FIRST NAME** OF THE MAN WHO DISCOVERED **ELECTRICITY?**

SMART ALECK: BEN WONDERING THAT MYSELF!

SOCIAL STUDIES TEACHER: WHAT DO **PEOPLE** IN THE **NETHERLANDS** WEAR ON THEIR **FEET?**

SMART ALECK: WOODEN SHOE LIKE TO KNOW!

SIMON: WHAT IS THE ***OUTSIDE PART*** OF A ***TREE CALLED?***

TEACHER: BARK!

SIMON: ***BOW-WOW!*** OK, NOW, WHAT IS THE ***OUTSIDE PART*** OF A ***TREE CALLED?***

WHEN DO YOU **TAKE** A ***SCHOOL TRIP?***

... IN THE ***FALL!***

POETRY CLASS

WHAT DO YOU CALL A STUDENT WHO ACES ALL HER TESTS?

A quiz whiz!

COUNSELOR CRACK UPS!

KELLI: I WANT TO BE A DOCTOR WHEN I GROW UP!

School Counselor: You have to have a lot of patients!

WHAT DID THE ***GOAT*** ORDER IN THE ***SCHOOL CAFETERIA?***

... ***BUTT***-ERED TOAST!

MUSIC TEACHER: WHAT KIND OF ***MUSIC*** DID THE ***PILGRIMS LIKE?***

JON: PLYMOUTH ROCK!

WHAT IS THE ***PAINTING TEACHER'S NAME?***

... ART N. CRAFTS!

TEACHER: WHICH **STATE** SELLS THE **MOST POTATOES?**

BILLY: I DUNNO!

TEACHER: THAT'S RIGHT!

MAD ADD JOKE!

MONEY
+ A CASHEW
DOUGH-NUT

School Nurse SICK JOKES

SALLY: A BUG JUST BIT MY TOE!

School Nurse: Which one?

SALLY: I DON'T KNOW. ALL BUGS LOOK ALIKE TO ME!

WHY DID THE ***STUDENT*** GET ***KICKED OUT*** OF ***MUSIC CLASS?***

... HE KEPT GETTING IN ***TREBLE!***

WHAT DID THE ***PITBULL*** GET IN THE ***SCHOOL PLAY?***

... A ***BIT*** PART!

WHAT'S THE ***WEIRDEST THING*** YOU'LL ***SEE*** IN THE ***SCHOOL CAFETERIA?***

... AN ***APPLE TURN OVER!***

SANDY: There's a dead fly in my soup!

Lunch Lady: Of course! Flies are bad swimmers!

WHICH ***SPORT*** DID THE ***EASTER BUNNY PLAY*** IN SCHOOL?

... ***BASKET***-BALL!

WHICH SPORT DO YELLOWJACKETS PLAY?
... FRIS-BEE!

WHICH ***SPORT*** IS ***ALWAYS*** GETTING IN ***TROUBLE?***

... ***BAD***-MINTON!

WHY WAS THE ***BASKETBALL TEAM UPSET*** WITH ITS ***TEAM PICTURE?***

... IT WAS A ***FOUL*** SHOT!

WHERE DO **COWS HANG THEIR ARTWORK** AT SCHOOL?

... ON THE **BULL**-ETIN BOARD!

WHAT **SPORT** DID THE **SHOE** PLAY IN SCHOOL?

... **SOCK**-ER!

WHY WASN'T THE COMPUTER ALLOWED TO DRIVE?
... BECAUSE IT KEPT CRASHING!

WHY WAS THE **COMPUTER** CALLED A **HERO?**

... BECAUSE IT WAS ALWAYS **SAVING** FILES!

WHICH LETTER IS MOST LIKE A BIRD?

J!

WHAT DID THE ***BUG*** SAY TO HER ***FRIEND?***
"WILL YOU HELP ME WITH MY ***MOTH HOMEWORK?***"

WHAT DO ***MUSIC TEACHERS*** LIKE TO ***WATCH ON TV?***

... CAR-***TUNES!***

WHY DID THE MUSIC TEACHER KEEP HER FLUTE IN THE REFRIGERATOR?
... SHE LIKED COOL MUSIC!
WHERE DO COMPUTERS GO ON SATURDAY NIGHT?
... TO THE DISK-O!
School Nurse
SICK JOKES
WHY DID THE DOG GO TO THE SCHOOL NURSE?
... It was feeling arf-ful!

WHAT DO YOU GET WHEN YOU **CROSS A MOSQUITO WITH A COMPUTER?**
... A LOT OF **BYTES!**

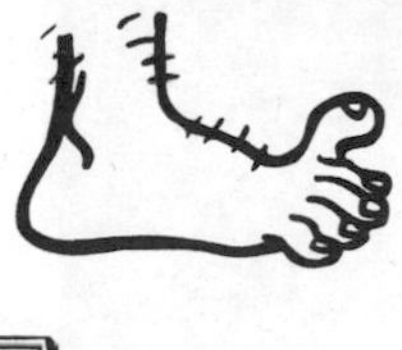

KELLI: IF I MAKE THE **STEP-DANCING TEAM,** I'M GONNA **STOMP** MY **FEET** FOR **JOY!**

WHAT KIND OF ***TEST*** DOES A ***DOG*** TAKE?

... A ***PUP*** QUIZ!

WHAT DID THE ***LUNCH LADY*** DO WHEN SHE WAS ***ANGRY?***
SHE GAVE EVERYONE A ***PIZZA*** HER MIND!

WHAT DO YOU CALL A ***GROUP OF ALIENS*** WHO ***PLAY INSTRUMENTS*** AS THEY ***WALK?***

... A SCHOOL ***MARTIAN*** BAND!

WHERE DID THE ***KING*** GO TO ***COLLEGE?***

... ***PRINCE***-TON!

MOM: DID YOU GET YOUR GRADE IN ITALIAN YET?
TOM: SI!
MOM: YOU CAN GET A BETTER GRADE THAN THAT!
WHAT DOES A KING USE TO MEASURE THINGS?
... A RULER!
SPIDER + PAW
BUG FOOT!
MAD ADD JOKE!

WHAT KIND OF ***SNAKES*** DO THEY SERVE IN THE ***SCHOOL CAFETERIA?***

... ***PIE***-THONS!

POETRY CLASS

WHAT'S ANOTHER NAME FOR A TEACHER'S ASSISTANT?

A grade aid!

ALEX: I'M GOING TO JOIN THE ***DRAMA CLUB*** AND ***ACT UP!***

TOM: THANK GOODNESS I ***WASN'T BORN*** IN ***SPAIN!***

MOM: WHY?

TOM: BECAUSE I GOT A ***"D"*** IN ***SPANISH CLASS!***

WHERE DO ***MOST LIBRARIANS COME FROM?***

... ***READING,*** PENNSYLVANIA!

WHAT INSTRUMENT WOULD A FISH PLAY IN THE MARCHING BAND?
... BASS!

WHY WAS THE GUM SAD?
... BECAUSE IT GOT CHEWED OUT IN CLASS!

GYM TEACHER: WHY DON'T YOU PRACTICE BASKETBALL WITH YOUR LITTLE SISTER?

FRED: SHE DOESN'T LIKE IT. BESIDES, I'D RATHER USE A REAL BASKETBALL!

KNOCK, KNOCK!
... WHO'S THERE?
IRISH!
... IRISH WHO?
IRISH I KNEW THE ANSWERS TO THIS TEST!

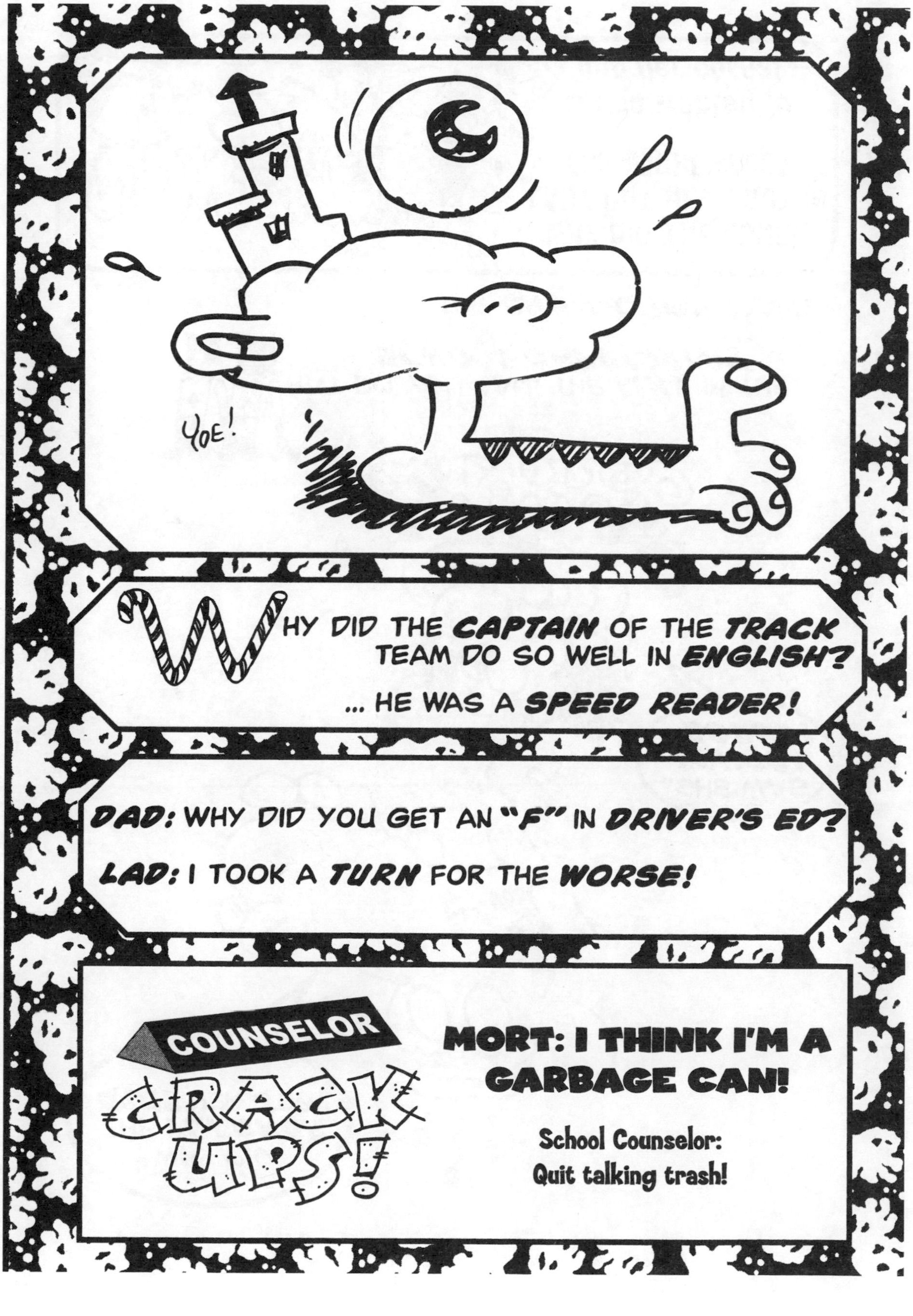
YOE!
WHY DID THE CAPTAIN OF THE TRACK TEAM DO SO WELL IN ENGLISH?
... HE WAS A SPEED READER!
DAD: WHY DID YOU GET AN "F" IN DRIVER'S ED?
LAD: I TOOK A TURN FOR THE WORSE!
COUNSELOR
CRACK UPS!
MORT: I THINK I'M A GARBAGE CAN!
School Counselor:
Quit talking trash!

WHAT DO YOU CALL THE ***LINE*** IN THE ***SCHOOL CAFETERIA?***

... THE ***CHEW-CHEW*** TRAIN!

WHY DID THE LUNCH LADY PUT HER FOOT IN THE MICROWAVE?

... She wanted to pop her corns!

SCHOOL NURSE: YOU **LOOK** VERY **TIRED!**

JAKE: YES, I STAYED UP ALL NIGHT **STUDYING** FOR MY **BLOOD TEST!**

WHAT IS A **SNOWMAN'S** FAVORITE **GRADE** IN SCHOOL?

... **FROST** GRADE!

THERESA: I WANT TO BE A ***TREE SURGEON*** WHEN I GROW UP!

SCHOOL COUNSLEOR: CAN YOU ***CUT*** IT?

WHY DID THE TEACHER SHOW THE CLASS THE ELEPHANT AT THE ZOO?
... THE LION WAS BUSY!

ZACK: I WANT TO BE A ***ZOOKEEPER*** WHEN I GROW UP!

SCHOOL COUNSELOR: IT'S A ***JUNGLE*** OUT THERE!

WHY DID THE ***GIANT*** GET IN ***TROUBLE*** AT SCHOOL?

... BECAUSE HE WAS TELLING ***TALL*** TALES!

PHIL: I'M THINKING OF TAKING DRIVER'S ED!
BILL: DO YOU THINK YOU AUTO?
WHY CAN'T YOU TAKE YOUR DOG TO SCHOOL?
... IT'S A NO BARKING ZONE!
YOE!
WHY DID THE LIGHTNING BUG GO TO THE SCHOOL NURSE?
... It had glowing pains!
School Nurse Sick Jokes

GEOGRAPHY TEACHER: WHICH ***CITY*** IS ***TILTED?***

SMART ALECK: NEW OR-***LEANS!***

WHAT KIND OF CHEESE DOES THE LUNCH LADY FEED HER DOG?
... MUTTS-ARELLA!
YOE!

WHAT ***PLAY*** DID THE ***DRAMA COACH ATTEND*** WITH HER ***CAT?***

... "THE SOUND OF ***MEOW***-SIC!"

MAD® ADD JOKE!

TREMBLE
\+ SHARP STICK

SHAKES-SPEAR!

TEACHER: FREDDY, IS THAT ***A BOOGER*** YOU'RE ***PULLING OUT OF YOUR NOSE?***

FREDDY: NO, IT'S ***SNOT!***

WHICH FOOTBALL POSITION DOES BARBED WIRE PLAY ON THE SCHOOL TEAM?
... DE-FENCE!

COACH: PHIL, DID YOU TAKE A ***SHOWER?***

PHIL: WHY? IS ONE ***MISSING?***

GEOGRAPHY TEACHER: WHICH ***CITY EATS*** THE MOST ***CHERRIES?***

SMART ALECK: ***PITTS***-BURGH!

WHAT DOES AN ***UMBRELLA ORDER*** WHEN THE CAFETERIA SERVES ***HAMBURGERS?***

... ***DRENCH*** FRIES!

WHAT DOES A ***WEIGHTLIFTER ORDER*** WHEN THE CAFETERIA SERVES ***HAMBURGERS?***

... ***BENCH*** FRIES!

WHAT DOES A ***THIRSTY KID ORDER*** WHEN THE CAFETERIA SERVES ***HAMBURGERS?***

... ***QUENCH*** FRIES!

WHICH LETTER IS THE OPPOSITE OF OUT?

N!

TODD: HELP! I NEED THE ***HEIMLICH MANEUVER!***

SCHOOL NURSE: ARE YOU ***CHOKING?***

TODD: WOULD I ***JOKE*** AT A ***TIME*** LIKE THIS?

WHAT KIND OF PETS DO TEACHERS AT BEAUTY SCHOOLS LIKE?
... HARES!
YOE!
POETRY CLASS
RHYME TIME!
WHAT DO HIGH SCHOOL STUDENTS WANT TO BE?
Glad grads!
WHICH SPORT DO GHOSTS PLAY IN SCHOOL?
... BOO-SKETBALL!

WHICH **SPORT** DO **INSECTS PLAY** IN SCHOOL?

... **BEE**-SKETBALL!

GEOGRAPHY TEACHER: WHICH **CITY** HAS THE MOST **BOATS?**

SMART ALECK: **OAR**-LANDO!

WHY DID THE ***BASEBALL PLAYER LEAVE*** THE FIELD?

... BECAUSE THE ***UMPIRE*** YELLED, ***"OUT!"***

WHY DID THE ***SCHOOL BASEBALL TEAM STOP WORKING?***

... BECAUSE THE ***UMPIRE*** YELLED, ***"STRIKE!"***

WHY DID THE ***PRINCIPAL*** BUY A ***CANARY*** INSTEAD OF A ***PARROT?***

... IT WAS ***CHEEP***-ER!

WHY DID THE ***LADDER FAIL*** HIS ***HISTORY TEST?***

... HE GOT THE ANSWERS ***RUNG!***

WHY DID THE ***MATH TEACHER*** WIN THE ***ARGUMENT*** WITH THE ***ENGLISH TEACHER?***

... BECAUSE ***FRACTIONS*** SPEAK ***LOUDER*** THAN ***WORDS!***

WHERE DOES THE LUNCH LADY'S KITTEN EAT?
... IN THE CAT-ETERIA!

WHAT DID THE ***DOG*** ORDER IN THE ***SCHOOL CAFETERIA?***

... ***POOCH***-ED EGGS!

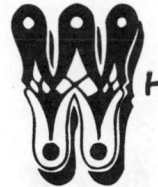

WHAT DO YOU ***LEARN*** FROM A ***TEACHER*** WHO TEACHES ***HEALTH*** AND ***MATH*** CLASSES?

... ***LUNG*** DIVISION!

WHAT ***SPORT*** DO ***PANCAKES PLAY*** AT ***SCHOOL?***

... ***BISCUIT***-BALL!

WHY DID THE ***TEACHER*** GO TO THE ***EYE DOCTOR?***

... SHE WAS HAVING ***TROUBLE*** WITH HER ***PUPILS!***

WHAT'S ***WRITTEN*** ABOVE THE ***DOOR*** OF A ***DOG OBEDIENCE SCHOOL?***

... THE ***SCHOOL MUTT-O!***

WHAT IS A MATH TEACHER'S FAVORITE DESSERT?
... PI!

WHAT ***TIME*** DOES ***SCHOOL START*** IN A ***CHICKEN COOP?***

... EIGHT O'***CLUCK!***

CHARLOTTE: I WANT TO JOIN THE ***SCHOOL CHORUS,*** BUT I'LL NEED A ***NOTE*** FROM MY MOTHER!

WHAT DOES A ***MATH TEACHER*** USE TO ***PLOW A FIELD?***

... A PRO-***TRACTOR!***

KENDALL: WHY ARE YOU ***GOING*** TO ***ENGLISH CLASS?***

ALEX: BECAUSE THE ***ENGLISH CLASS*** WON'T ***COME*** TO ME!

WHERE DOES AN AVERAGE STUDENT GO ON VACATION?
... C-WORLD!
YOE!

WHAT DO YOU SAY WHEN THE ***LUNCH LADY*** GIVES YOU A ***HOT DOG?***

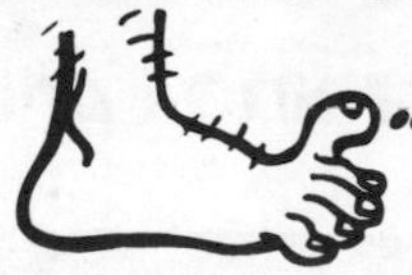

... "***FRANKS*** A LOT!"

COUNSELOR CRACK UPS!

TIM: EVERYBODY IGNORES ME!

School Counselor: Next!

Yearbook Yuks!

WHERE CAN YOU FIND YOUR ***BUTT'S*** CLASS ***PICTURE?***

... IN A **REARBOOK!**

WHERE CAN YOU FIND A ***COW'S*** CLASS ***PICTURE?***

... IN A **STEERBOOK!**

WHERE CAN YOU FIND ***FRANKENSTEIN'S*** CLASS ***PICTURE?***

... IN A **FEARBOOK!**

WHERE CAN YOU FIND ***BAMBI'S*** CLASS ***PICTURE?***

... IN A **DEERBOOK!**

WHERE CAN YOU FIND A ***MECHANIC'S*** CLASS ***PICTURE?***

... IN A **GEARBOOK!**

WHERE CAN YOU FIND AN ***EAR'S*** CLASS ***PICTURE?***

... IN A **HEARBOOK!**

WHERE CAN YOU FIND A ***FORTUNE TELLER'S*** CLASS ***PICTURE?***

... IN A **SEERBOOK!**

WHERE CAN YOU FIND A ***SAD PERSON'S*** CLASS ***PICTURE?***

... IN A **TEARBOOK!**

WHERE CAN YOU FIND A ***LOOKING GLASS'S*** CLASS ***PICTURE?***

... IN A **MIRRORBOOK!**

WHERE CAN YOU FIND A ***PEEPING TOM'S*** CLASS ***PICTURE?***

... IN A **LEERBOOK!**

WHERE CAN YOU FIND A ***FELLOW STUDENT'S*** CLASS ***PICTURE?***

... IN A **PEERBOOK!**

WHAT IS A ***GIRL'S*** FAVORITE ***SCHOOL SUBJECT?***

... ***HER***-STORY!

WHAT IS A ***PIG'S*** FAVORITE ***SCHOOL SUBJECT?***
... ***STY***-ENCE!

WHY DID THE ***TEACHER*** PUT ***CAT LITTER*** IN THE ***CLASSROOM?***

... FOR THE ***TEACHER'S PET!***

WHY ARE ***ANESTHESIOLOGISTS*** GOOD AT ***MATH?***

... BECAUSE OF ALL THE ***NUMB***-ERS!

WHAT DO YOU GET WHEN YOU CROSS A POLICE OFFICER WITH THE LUNCH LADY?

... Captain Cook!

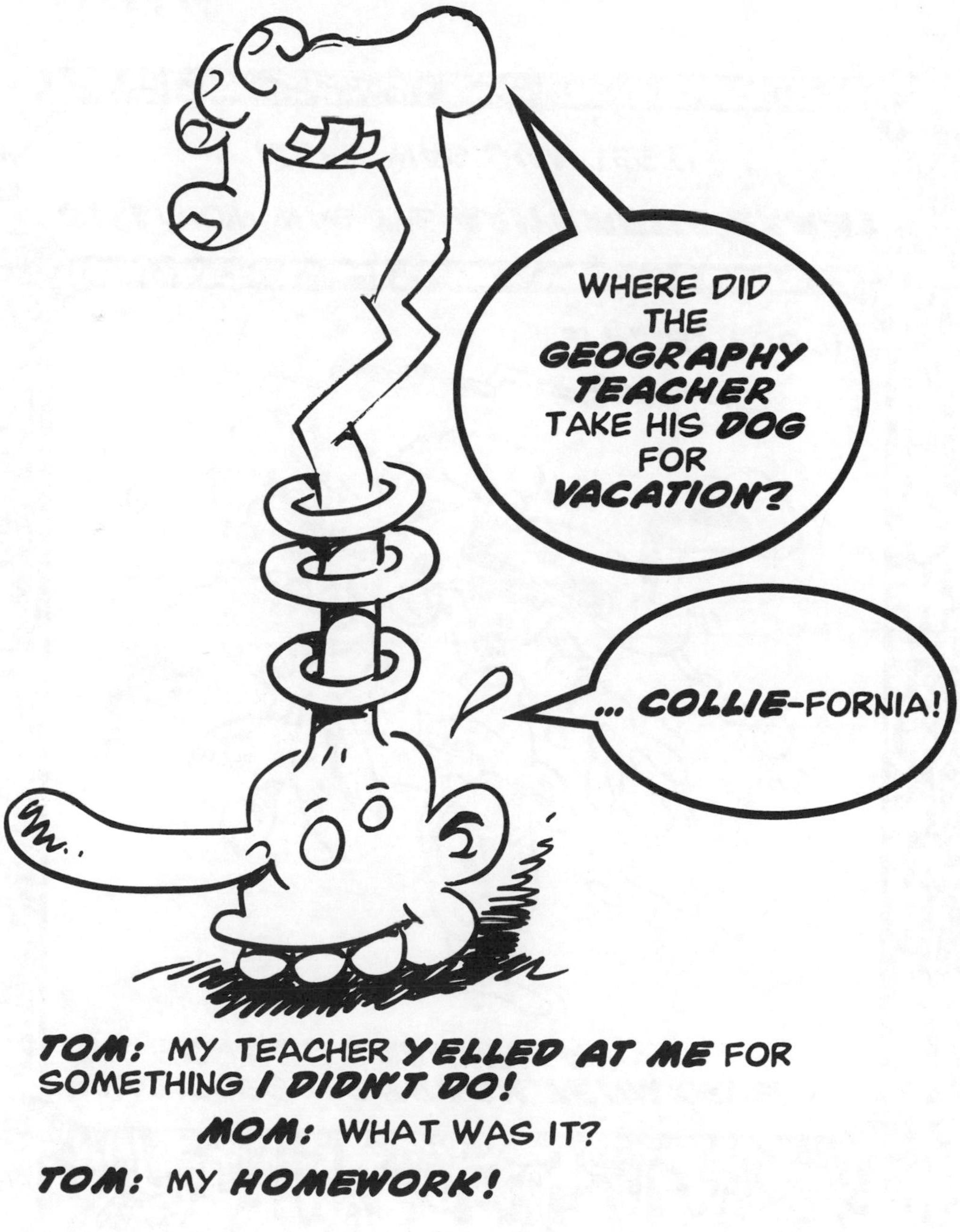

WHERE DID THE GEOGRAPHY TEACHER TAKE HIS DOG FOR VACATION?
... COLLIE-FORNIA!

TOM: MY TEACHER ***YELLED AT ME*** FOR SOMETHING ***I DIDN'T DO!***

MOM: WHAT WAS IT?

TOM: MY ***HOMEWORK!***

WHAT DOES THE ***TRACK TEAM*** ORDER IN THE ***SCHOOL CAFETERIA?***

... ***FAST*** FOOD!

JILL: HOW WAS THE ***ARITHMETIC EXAM?***

LIL: IT WAS ***SUM*** TEST!

MAD® ADD JOKE!

SODIUM
+ EYEBALL
———————
SALT AND PEEPER

WHAT WILL HAPPEN IF YOU ***DON'T PASS*** YOUR ***HISTORY CLASS?***

... HISTORY WILL REPEAT ITSELF!

WHAT DID THE ***BUG ORDER*** IN THE ***SCHOOL CAFETERIA?***

... ***LICE*** KRISPIES!

WHAT ***CAN'T YOU HAVE*** UNTIL ***IT'S TAKEN?***

... YOUR SCHOOL PICTURE!

TOM: I ***FAILED EVERY SUBJECT*** EXCEPT ***GEOMETRY!***

MOM: HOW DID YOU DO ***THAT?***

TOM: I DIDN'T TAKE GEOMETRY!

WHICH ***SPORT*** WOULD AN ***INSECT PLAY*** IN SCHOOL?

... CRICKET!

WHAT DOES THE **LUNCH LADY FEED HER CAT?**
...UNCLE BEN'S **MICE!**
YOE!

WHAT DO YOU CALL ***SOMEONE*** WHO WEARS A ***UNIFORM,*** CARRIES ***POM-POMS,*** AND IS ALWAYS ***INSULTING PEOPLE?***

... A ***JEER***-LEADER!

WHAT DO YOU CALL A STUDENT WHO CAN DRAW WELL?

Art smart!

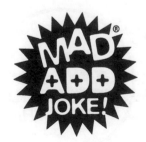

WHAT DO YOU CALL ***SOMEONE*** WHO WEARS A ***UNIFORM***, CARRIES ***POM-POMS***, AND IS ALWAYS ***CRYING?***

... A ***TEAR***-LEADER!

WHAT DID THE TEACHER'S DOG SAY TO THE FLEA?
... "GO AWAY! YOU'RE BUGGING ME!"
YOE!

MAD ADD JOKE!

KRIS KRINGLE
+ A BEAR

SANTA CLAWS

WHAT KIND OF ***PET*** WOULD THE ***SCIENCE TEACHER*** HAVE IF HE ***CROSSED*** A ***PIG*** WITH A ***GERBIL?***

... A ***HAM***-STER!

TEACHER: WHO CAN TELL ME WHAT WAS ***WORN*** DURING THE ***BOSTON TEA PARTY?***

TOM: TEA-SHIRTS!

PRINCIPAL: IS THE **SCHOOL CHOIR IMPROVING?**

MUSIC TEACHER: YES. **PEOPLE** ARE ONLY **COVERING ONE EAR** NOW!

HOW DO **HORNETS** GET TO SCHOOL?

... THEY TAKE THE SCHOOL ***BUZZ!***

TEACHER: DO YOU HAVE ***SOMETHING*** IN YOUR ***NOSE?***

ALVIN: NO. I'M ***TRYING*** TO ***SMELL*** THE ***TIP*** OF MY ***FINGER!***

WHY DID THE FROG STUDY ALL NIGHT?
YOE!
... HE WAS SWAMPED WITH HOMEWORK!

TEACHER: HOW MANY ***DAYS*** OF THE ***WEEK*** END IN ***Y?***

SMART ALECK: EIGHT—MONDAY, TUESDAY, WEDNESDAY, THURSDAY, FRIDAY, SATURDAY, SUNDAY, AND ***YESTERDAY!***

WHAT DO YOU CALL A GROUP OF KIDS WHO EAT TOGETHER IN THE CAFETERIA?

A lunch bunch!

TEACHER'S PET

PART I

WHEN THE ***BASKETBALL COACH*** TAKES HIS ***DOG CAMPING,*** WHERE DO THEY ***SLEEP?***

... IN A ***PUP*** TENT!

WHICH ***KIND OF PET*** DOES THE ***SCHOOL NURSE*** HAVE?

... A FIRST AID KIT-TEN!

WHY CAN THE ***MUSIC TEACHER*** AFFORD ***12 CANARIES?***

... HE GOT THEM FOR ***A SONG!***

WHAT DOES THE ***GYM TEACHER*** PLAY WITH HIS ***PUPPY?***

... DOG ***TAG!***

WHAT DID THE ***LUNCH LADY*** USE TO MAKE HER DOG ***COOKIES?***

... ***COLLIE*** FLOUR!

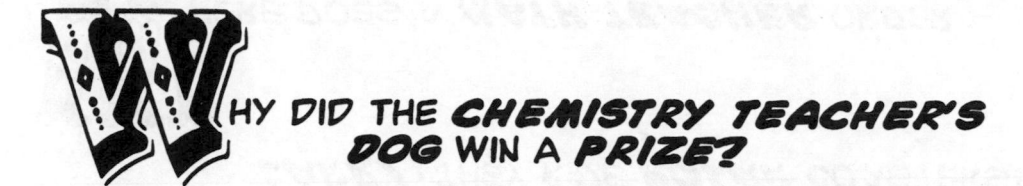

WHY DID THE ***CHEMISTRY TEACHER'S DOG*** WIN A ***PRIZE?***

... HE WAS THE MOST ***PUP***-ULAR!

WHAT DO YOU CALL ***GLOVES*** FOR A ***DOG?***

... ***MUTTENS!***

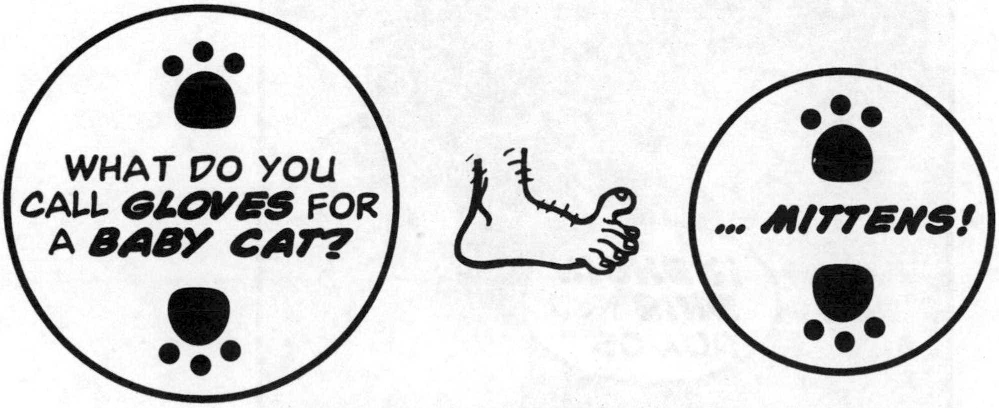

WHAT DO YOU CALL GLOVES FOR A BABY CAT?
... MITTENS!

WHY DID THE ***ART TEACHER*** HAVE HIS ***PUPPY*** SWALLOW A ***CLOCK?***

... HE WANTED A ***WATCH DOG!***

SOCIAL STUDIES TEACHER: WHAT DO **PENGUINS** DO FOR **FUN?**

LARRY: THEY RIDE **POLAR** COASTERS!

WHERE DOES A **MATH TEACHER** ORDER HER **LUNCH?**

... AT THE **COUNTER!**

WHERE DO THEY HOLD ***WEIRD*** SCHOOL ***PLAYS?***

... IN THE ***ODD***-ITORIUM!

WHAT DID THE FROG SAY WHEN HE GOT A HAMBURGER?

... "Can I have flies with that?"

MATH TEACHER: IF YOU **SAVED ONE DOLLAR** EVERY **DAY** FOR A **MONTH,** WHAT WOULD YOU **GET?**

JOHN: A NEW **VIDEO GAME!**

COUNSELOR CRACK UPS!

FRED: WILL YOU HELP ME OUT?

School Counselor: Which way did you come in?

WHAT HAPPENED WHEN THE ***OMELET ACTED UP*** IN SCHOOL?

 ... IT GOT ***EGGS***-PELLED!

WHAT'S THE MOST ***STRESSFUL PART*** OF SCHOOL?

... DE-***TENSION!***

WHERE DID ***SIR LANCELOT*** EARN HIS ***DIPLOMA?***

... IN ***KNIGHT*** SCHOOL!

WHY DID THE GIRL SIGN UP FOR HISTORY CLASS?
... SHE WANTED TO GET SOME DATES!

WHY DID THE ***CLOCK GET IN TROUBLE*** IN CLASS?

... BECAUSE IT ***TOCKED*** TOO MUCH!

WHY DID THE ***TEACHER*** START ***DATING*** THE ***JANITOR?***

... HE ***SWEPT*** HER OFF HER FEET!

WHY DID THE ***BIG CAT*** GET AN "***F***" ON HIS ***REPORT?***

... BECAUSE HE WAS A ***CHEETAH!***

MAD ADD JOKE!

NOT DR. JEKYLL
\+ BIRD'S MOUTH

HYDE AND BEAK

TEACHER: SPELL "**CAT.**"

JAYNE: C-A!

TEACHER: ALMOST. WHAT'S AT THE **END?**

JAYNE: IT'S **TAIL!**

School Nurse Sick Jokes

WHY DID THE CLOWN GO TO THE SCHOOL NURSE?

Because he felt funny!

WHY DID THE ***TEACHER*** HAVE ***BAD MANNERS?***

... SHE HAD ***NO CLASS!***

TERRY: I'M GOING TO ***JOIN*** THE ***YEARBOOK COMMITTEE.*** IT'LL BE ***PICTURE PERFECT!***

WHY DO **SOCCER PLAYERS** DO WELL IN **SCHOOL?**

... THEY'RE ALWAYS USING THEIR **HEADS!**

GEOGRAPHY TEACHER: WHICH **CITY** IS THE **WEALTHIEST?**

SMART ALECK: RICH-MOND!

WHICH **SCHOOL TEAM** DO **COWS** PLAY ON?

... THE BASE-**BULL** TEAM!

POETRY CLASS

WHAT DO YOU CALL A QUESTION ABOUT THE CIVIL WAR THAT YOU CAN'T ANSWER?

A history mystery!

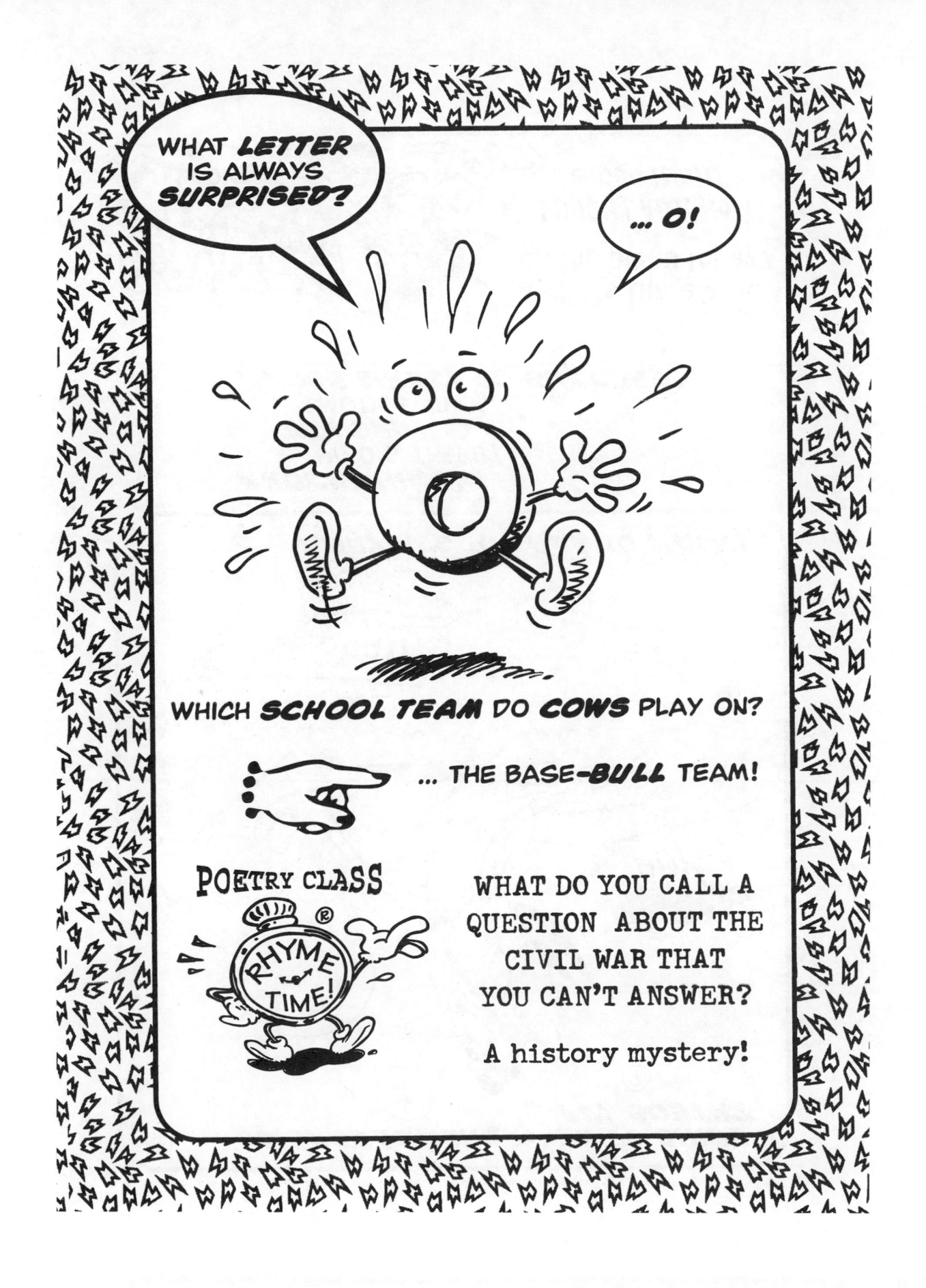

KNOCK-KNOCK!

WHO'S THERE?

MOOSE!

MOOSE WHO?

MOOSE LIKELY TO SUCCEED!

PHIL: Is there stew on the menu today?

LUNCH LADY: No, I wiped it off!

WHAT DO THEY ***SERVE*** IN THE ***CAFETERIA IN SORCERY SCHOOLS?***

... SAND-***WITCHES!***

WHY DID THE EGG GET THROWN OUT OF CLASS?
... BECAUSE HE KEPT TELLING YOLKS!

WHY DID THE ***CAPTAIN*** OF THE ***BASKETBALL TEAM*** EAT ***COOKIES AND MILK?***

... HE LIKED TO ***DUNK!***

WHY DID THE ***FROG*** MAKE THE ***SCHOOL BASEBALL TEAM?***

... HE WAS GOOD AT ***CATCHING FLIES!***

BOB: I'M TAKING AN **ASTRONOMY CLASS!**

ROB: YOU'LL JUST BE TAKING UP **SPACE!**

WHAT DID THE MECHANIC GIVE TO HIS PROM DATE?
... A CAR-SAGE!

ANNMARIE: I WANT TO JOIN THE **MATH CLUB.** IT'LL BE A LOT OF FUN, **I FIGURE!**

WHAT DO **PENGUINS RIDE** TO SCHOOL?

... THEIR B-**ICE**-CYCLES!

MONSTER: HOW'S MY **EYESIGHT?**

SCHOOL NURSE: YOU HAVE **20-20-20-20 VISION!**

MATH TEACHER: WHICH **NUMBER** ISN'T **HUNGRY?**

SMART ALECK: 8!

MAD ADD JOKE!

SNOWMAN
+ BANDAGES
FROST AID KIT

MATH TEACHER: BRING A ***POCKET CALCULATOR*** TO ***CLASS*** TOMORROW.

BILLY: WHAT IF WE ALREADY KNOW HOW MANY ***POCKETS*** WE HAVE?

COUNSELOR CRACK UPS!

MARIA: WHEN I GROW UP I WANT TO WORK IN A BANK!

School Counselor: There's a lot of money in that!

WHAT IS THE ***LAZIEST*** THING IN THE ***CAFETERIA?***

... THE ***NAP***-KINS!

WHAT IS THE ***COOLEST FOOD*** IN THE ***CAFETERIA?***

... THE ***RAD***-ISHES!

WHAT DO ***SNOWMEN*** ORDER IN THEIR ***SALADS?***

... CUCUM-***BRRRRS!***

WHY DID THE BANANA GET VOTED PROM QUEEN?
... SHE HAD A LOT OF AP-PEEL!

WHAT DO YOU DO WHEN A ***PIG CHOKES*** IN THE ***SCHOOL CAFETERIA?***

... YOU GIVE HIM THE ***HAM-LICH MANEUVER!***

WHY DID THE TEACHER ***YELL*** AT THE ***COCOA?***

... BECAUSE IT WAS CHOCO-***LATE!***

TEACHER: STU, WHAT'S THE ***ENGLISH CHANNEL?***

STU: I DON'T KNOW. WE ***DON'T*** HAVE ***CABLE!***

POETRY CLASS

WHAT DO YOU CALL A SCHOOL GYMNASIUM WITH POOR LIGHTING?

A dim gym!

WHAT DO YOU GET WHEN YOU CROSS A SCHOOL JANITOR WITH A CHEERLEADER?
... A CHORE-LEADER!
YOE!
TOM: I HEARD THE MUSIC TEACHER IS SELLING HIS VIOLIN - NO STRINGS ATTACHED!
MAD® ADD JOKE!
RABBIT
+ ANGER
HOPPING MAD

WHICH ***PART*** OF A ***DESK*** IS AN ***ART TEACHER'S*** FAVORITE?

... THE ***DRAW***-ERS!

WHAT SHOULD YOU USE TO BLOW YOUR NOSE IN THE CAFETERIA?
... DISH-UES!

WHO ***RUNS THE SCHOOL*** AND IS ALSO YOUR ***BEST FRIEND?***

... THE PRINCI-***PAL!***

WHERE DO ***DISHONEST*** PEOPLE GO TO ***STUDY?***

... THE ***LIE***-BRARY!

MOM: HOW DID YOU GET AN ***"F"*** ON YOUR ***REPORT ON DOLPHINS?***

TOM: I DIDN'T DO IT ON ***PORPOISE!***

WHERE DO ***BIRDS*** KEEP THEIR ***BOOKS AT SCHOOL?***

... IN THEIR ***FLOCKERS!***

JOHNNY: I'M GOING TO ***JOIN*** THE ***ART CLUB.*** IT'S A BIG ***DRAW!***

WHAT IS ***HERCULES'*** FAVORITE ***SUBJECT?***

... ***MYTHMATICS*** CLASS!

WHY DID THE KANGAROO GO TO THE SCHOOL NURSE?

It wanted to find out if it needed a hop-eration!

TEACHER: HOW DO YOU SPELL "***WEATHER***"?

TOM: W-E-T-H-U-R!

TEACHER: THAT'S THE ***WORST SPELL*** OF ***WEATHER*** WE'VE HAD IN YEARS!

TIMMY: What's this fly doing in my soup?

LUNCH LADY: The backstroke!

WHEN DO ***BOXERS*** EAT WHILE THEY'RE AT ***SCHOOL?***

... AT ***PUNCH*** TIME!

PRINCIPAL: I UNDERSTAND YOU WERE ***MISBEHAVING*** ON THE ***PLAYGROUND EQUIPMENT!***

HARRY: YES, SIR, BUT COULDN'T YOU LET IT ***SLIDE?***

WHICH CLASS IS A BORED PERSON'S FAVORITE?
... SIGH-ENCE!

HAT DOES A ***WINDOW*** USE TO ***TAKE NOTES?***

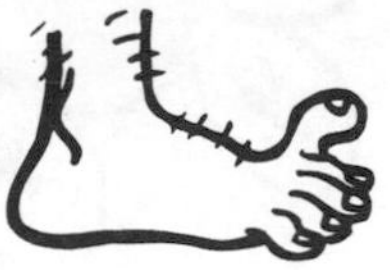

... A PEN-***SILL!***

MAD® ADD JOKE!

DINOSAUR
+ LARGEST STATE
TYRANNOSAURUS TEX

TOM: I NEED AN **ENCYCLOPEDIA!**

MOM: YOU CAN **RIDE** A **BICYCLE** TO **SCHOOL** JUST LIKE EVERYONE **ELSE!**

WHAT SHOULD YOU USE TO **FIND YOUR WAY** IF YOU GET LOST IN **MATH CLASS?**
... A **COMPASS!**

WHY DID THE ***ALGEBRA TEACHER*** GO TO THE ***BEAUTICIAN?***

... HER ***SQUARE ROOTS*** WERE SHOWING!

WHAT ***INSTRUMENT*** WOULD A ***TURKEY*** PLAY IN THE ***MARCHING BAND?***

... ***DRUMS,*** BECAUSE HE HAS ***THE DRUMSTICKS!***

WHICH ***TEACHER*** NEEDS THE MOST ***SUBSTITUTES?***

... THE MU-***SICK***-TEACHER!

COUNSELOR CRACK UPS!

TOM: I THINK I'M A DECK OF CARDS!

School Counselor: Deal with it!

WHERE DO YOU ***LEARN*** TO ***SWIM?***

... IN ***DIVER'S ED!***

WHAT ***INSTRUMENT*** WOULD A ***ROOF*** PLAY IN THE ***SCHOOL BAND?***

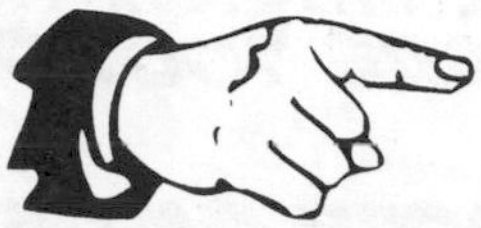

... GUI-***TAR!***

WHAT ***INSTRUMENT*** WOULD A ***DOG*** PLAY IN THE ***SCHOOL BAND?***

... TROM-***BONE!***

POLICE OFFICER: ALL THE **KIDS FELL OUT** OF YOUR **BUS TWO BLOCKS BACK!**

SCHOOL BUS DRIVER: OH, THANK YOU! I THOUGHT I HAD **BECOME DEAF!**

WHAT KIND OF **PEOPLE** DOES THE **SCHOOL LIBRARIAN DISLIKE?**

... BOOK-KEEPERS!

WHAT DO YOU CALL SOMEONE WHO WEARS A *UNIFORM, CARRIES POM-POMS,* AND *LOVES BOOKS?*
... A *CHEER-READER!*

WHAT DO YOU CALL SOMEONE WHO WEARS A ***UNIFORM, CARRIES POM-POMS,*** AND ***WORKS IN A GARDEN?***

... A ***CHEER-WEEDER!***

School Nurse
SICK JOKES

WHY DID DRACULA GO TO THE SCHOOL NURSE?

... Because he was coffin!

MATH TEACHER: HOW ***LONG*** IS YOUR ***SHOE?***

SMART ALECK: ONE ***FOOT!***

FOWL
+ DOG
+ BROTH

CHICKEN POODLE SOUP

WHY DID THE ***TENNIS TEAM*** GET IN TROUBLE?

... THEY WERE MAKING A ***RACKET!***

MUSIC TEACHER: IF YOU ***DON'T STOP*** PRACTICING THE ***CYMBALS*** I'M GOING TO GO ***NUTS!***

MIKE: TOO LATE. I STOPPED ***TWO HOURS AGO!***

WHERE DO ***FUTURE IRS WORKERS*** SPEND THEIR TIME IN ***SCHOOL?***

... THE ***AUDIT***-ORIUM!

SCIENCE TEACHER: WHAT DO YOU CALL AN **OBJECT** THAT **FLIES** THROUGH **SPACE** LEAVING A **TAIL** BEHIND IT?

BRITNEY: I CAN'T **COMET!**

POETRY CLASS

WHERE DOES A MEMBER OF THE BAND KEEP HIS OR HER BOOKS?

In a rocker locker!

WHY DID THE ***CAT*** PERFORM ***BADLY*** IN ***DANCE CLASS?***

... BECAUSE IT HAD ***TWO LEFT FEET!***

WHAT DID ***PRESIDENT LINCOLN*** LEARN IN ***SCHOOL?***

... THE ***ABE,*** B, C'S!

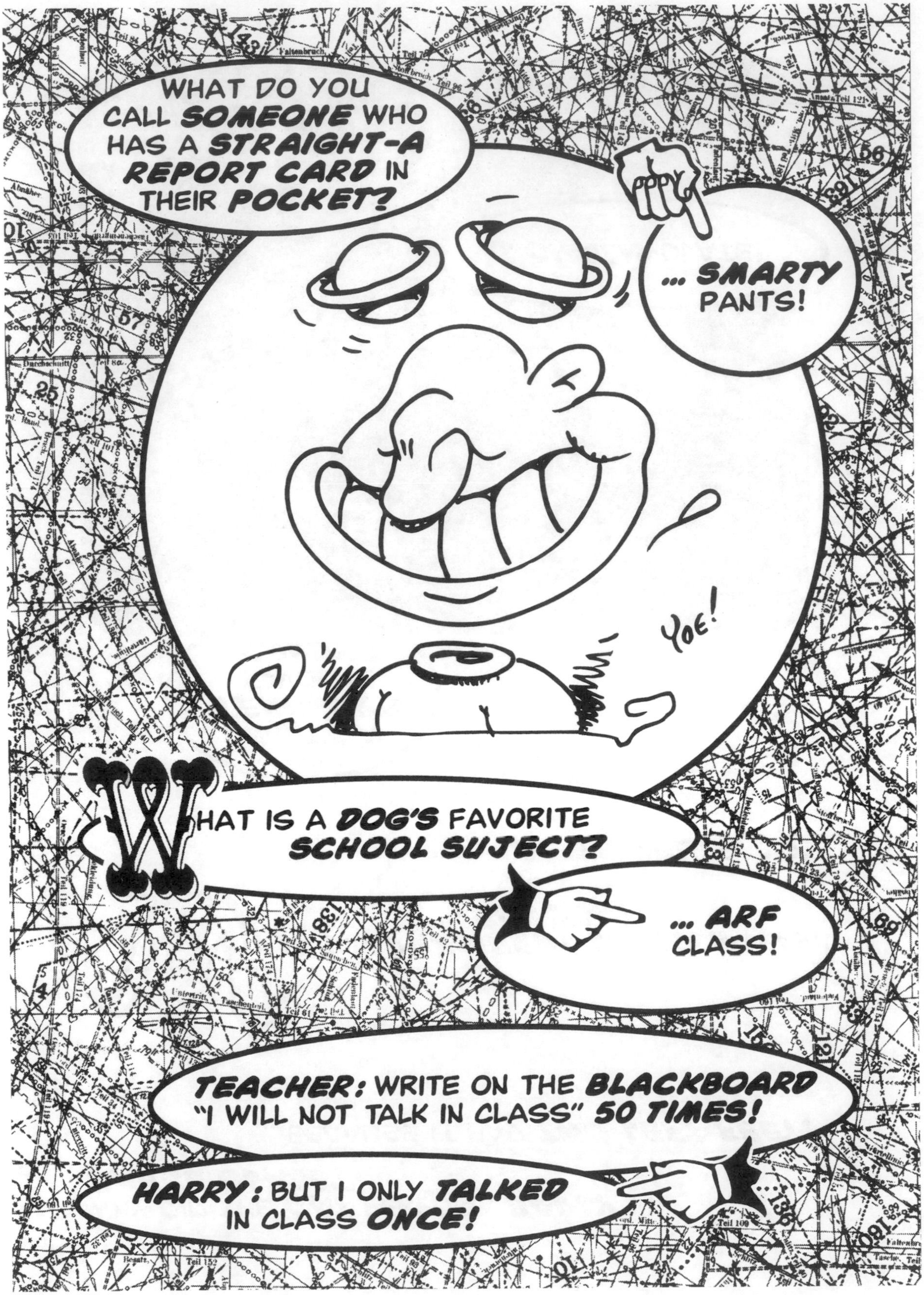
WHAT DO YOU CALL SOMEONE WHO HAS A STRAIGHT-A REPORT CARD IN THEIR POCKET?
... SMARTY PANTS!
YOE!
WHAT IS A DOG'S FAVORITE SCHOOL SUJECT?
... ARF CLASS!
TEACHER: WRITE ON THE BLACKBOARD "I WILL NOT TALK IN CLASS" 50 TIMES!
HARRY: BUT I ONLY TALKED IN CLASS ONCE!

SCIENCE TEACHER: WHERE CAN YOU FIND THE ***LARGEST DIAMOND?***

DEREK: IN A ***BASEBALL STADIUM!***

WHICH KIND OF BOOKS DO THEY READ IN DALLAS?
... TEX BOOKS!

WHY DID THE BOY ***SWALLOW THE DOLLAR BILL*** HIS MOTHER GAVE HIM?

... SHE TOLD HIM IT WAS ***LUNCH MONEY!***

WHAT HAPPENED WHEN THE ***ART TEACHER*** SUBSTITUTED FOR THE ***FOOTBALL COACH?***

... HE TAUGHT THE TEAM HOW TO ***PUNT BY NUMBERS!***

WHAT DOES ***SPAGHETTI PLAY*** IN ***GYM CLASS?***

... ***MEAT***-BALL!

SAL: THERE ARE TIMES WHEN I DON'T ***FEEL LIKE EATING*** AT ALL.

HAL: WHEN?

SAL: RIGHT AFTER ***LUNCH!***

MILLIE: This hamburger tastes funny!

***LUNCH LADY:* Made you laugh!**

GEOGRAPHY TEACHER: WHICH ***CITY*** LENDS A LOT OF ***MONEY?***

GEORGE: BARCE-***LOAN***-A!

WHO IS AN ***ENGLISH TEACHER'S*** FAVORITE ***RELATIVE?***

... HIS ***GRAMMAR!***

MATH CLASS
+ ENGLISH CLASS

ADD-VERB

SCIENCE TEACHER: HOW DO YOU TELL AN **OSTRICH** FROM AN **AARDVARK?**

KELLI: AN **OSTRICH** DOESN'T LOOK LIKE AN **AARDVARK!**

WHY WAS THE ***BOOK SCARED?***

... IT WAS ***SPINELESS!***

WHAT NUMBER LIKES TO SUN ITSELF ON THE BEACH?
... 10!

WHAT ***TEAM*** DO ***LAZY STUDENTS*** JOIN?

... THE ***REST***-LING TEAM!

SCIENCE TEACHER: WHY AREN'T THERE ***DOGS*** ON ***MARS?***

JAYNE: BECAUSE THERE AREN'T ANY ***FIRE HYDRANTS!***

WHY DID THE ***SPIDER*** TAKE THE ***COMPUTER CLASS?***

... SO IT COULD SURF THE ***WEB!***

COUNSELOR CRACK UPS!

MELVIN: I THINK I'M A SNAIL!

School Counselor: You really need to come out of your shell!

WHERE DO ***KIDS IN PARIS*** GO ON ***FRIDAY NIGHT?***

 ... TO THE ***SCHOOL FRANCE!***

WHERE DO ***YOUNG HYPNOTISTS*** GO ON ***FRIDAY NIGHT?***

... TO THE ***SCHOOL TRANCE!***

SCIENCE TEACHER: WHAT'S ***GREEN*** AND HAS ***HAIRY EYEBALLS*** AND ***TWO PINCHERS?***

CLIZIA: I DON'T KNOW.

SCIENCE TEACHER: I DON'T KNOW EITHER, BUT THERE'S ONE ***CRAWLING*** ON YOUR ***NECK!***

WHAT DO THE STOOGES EAT IN THE SCHOOL CAFETERIA?
... MOE, LARRY, AND CURLY FRIES!
MOM: WHAT DO YOU MEAN I HAVE TO WEAR A SNORKEL TO LOOK AT YOUR REPORT CARD?
HANNAH: MY GRADES ARE UNDER C LEVEL!
School Nurse
SICK JOKES
WHAT DID THE SCHOOL NURSE DO WHEN THE MOUSE FAINTED?
She gave him mouth-to-mouse resuscitation!

WHAT DOES A ***WHINY KID*** RIDE
TO SCHOOL?

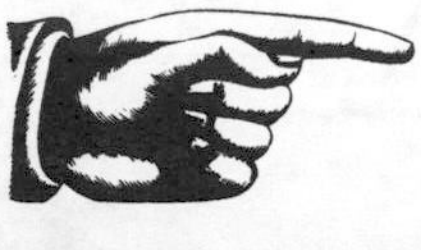

... THE SCHOOL ***FUSS!***

WHY DID THE ***SMALL BUCKET*** GO ***SEE***
THE ***SCHOOL NURSE?***

... IT WAS ***LOOKING*** A LITTLE ***PAIL!***

WHAT IS A ***TAILOR'S***
FAVORITE ***SUBJECT?***

... ***SEW***-CIAL STUDIES!

SCHOOL NEWSPAPER EDITOR: THE **SCHOOL CAFETERIA** IS NOW SERVING **ICE-CREAM CONES** – LET'S GET THE **SCOOP!**

MAD ADD JOKE!

MINERALS
+ OCEAN
VITAMIN SEA

GEOGRAPHY TEACHER: WHICH ***BODY*** OF ***WATER*** DO YOU FIND ***BETWEEN*** THE ***ATLANTIC*** AND ***PACIFIC OCEANS?***

SMART ALECK: TENNE-***SEA!***

WHICH STATE DID THE GEOGRAPHY TEACHER SAY IS MOST LIKE YOUR LEG?
... KNEE-BRASKA!

MATH TEACHER: IF YOU TAKE ***THREE*** FROM ***SEVEN,*** WHAT'S THE ***DIFFERENCE?***

STAN: WHAT DO YOU MEAN "WHAT'S THE ***DIFFERENCE"?*** TEACHER, I THINK YOU HAVE A ***BAD ATTITUDE!***

YOE!
WHICH DRINK IS FOUND IN THE ALPHABET?
... TEA!
HOW DOES A CHEERLEADER MAKE PHONE CALLS?
... ON HER YELL PHONE!
MAD ADD JOKE!
GRIDLOCK + JELLY
TRAFFIC JAM

WHO IS THE ***CRABBIEST PERSON*** YOU ***SEE*** WHEN YOU ***WALK*** TO ***SCHOOL?***

... THE ***CROSS***-ING GUARD!

WHY DID THE REFRIGERATOR TRY OUT FOR THE TRACK TEAM?
... IT WAS ALWAYS RUNNING!

WHAT ROLE WOULD A ***PRISONER*** PLAY IN THE ***SCHOOL BAND?***

... ***CON***-DUCTOR!

WHY DID EVERYONE IN CLASS HAVE TO GET ***BANDAGES?***

... THEY WENT ON A SCHOOL ***TRIP!***

WHAT'S ***LOUDER*** THAN A ***CHEERLEADER?***

... TWO CHEERLEADERS!

FREDDY: What's for lunch today?

LUNCH LADY:* *The stuff no one wanted yesterday!

WHAT DOES A ***PIG*** DO ***AFTER SCHOOL?***

... ***HAM*** WORK!

SUE: YOU'RE THE ***BEST DANCER*** AT THE ***PROM*** EXCEPT FOR ***TWO THINGS!***

LOU: WHAT'S THAT?

SUE: YOUR ***FEET!***

MELVIN: I WANT TO TAKE A ***DRIVER'S ED CLASS!***

DRIVER'S ED TEACHER: I WON'T ***STAND*** IN YOUR ***WAY!***

HOW DO YOU SPELL ***"TEACHER"*** BACKWARDS?

... ***T-E-A-C-H-E-R-B-A-C-K-W-A-R-D-S!***

WHICH PART OF YOUR EYE GOES TO SCHOOL?
... THE PUPIL!

WHICH IS THE ***BIGGEST PUNCTUATION MARK?***

... THE ***50-YARD DASH!***

MAD ADD JOKE!

DINER
+ CHEERLEADER

RESTAU-RAH-RAH-RAH-NT

WHAT IS A ***SHOPPER'S*** FAVORITE CLASS?

... ***BUY***-OLOGY!

KATHY: WHAT'S ON THE **MENU** TODAY?

LUNCH LADY: THOUSANDS OF **THINGS.**

KATHY: WHAT?

LUNCH LADY: LIMA BEANS!

WHICH SUBJECT IS A MOUSE'S FAVORITE?
... LITE-RAT-URE!
YOE!

MAD® ADD JOKE!

YELLOW VEGGIE
+ POLICE OFFICER

CORN ON THE COP

WHAT DO YOU CALL THE SCHOOL COACH WITH GRAPE JELLY SPREAD ON HIM?
... THE JAM TEACHER!
WHY DID THE PIG GET THE LEAD PART IN THE SCHOOL PLAY?
... BECAUSE HE WAS A BIG HAM!
TEACHER: FREDDY, I CAN READ YOUR ENGLISH PAPER, BUT YOUR MATH HOMEWORK IS ILLEGIBLE!
FREDDY: MY BROTHER WRITES MUCH SLOPPIER THAN MY SISTER!

WHICH POSITION WOULD A PERSON WHO'S NEVER WRONG PLAY ON THE SCHOOL BASEBALL TEAM?
... RIGHT FIELD!
WHAT KIND OF SUNTAN LOTION DOES A JANITOR WEAR?
... MOP-ERTONE!
COUNSELOR
CRACK UPS!
JIM: NOBODY TAKES ME SERIOUSLY.
School Counselor: Ha, ha, ha, ha, ha!

WAYNE: I THINK I'M A **CAT!**

SCHOOL NURSE: HOW **LONG** HAS THIS BEEN **GOING ON?**

WAYNE: SINCE I WAS A **KITTEN!**

WHAT IS A COMPUTER'S FAVORITE MUSICAL INSTRUMENT?
... THE KEYBOARD!

AH-CHOO!!

HAT'S THE **BEST THING** TO DO ON A **LAZY DAY?**

... GO TO THE **SCHOOL CAFETERIA** AND WATCH THE **MEAT LOAF!**

WHAT DID THE LIBRARIAN SAY WHEN THE VEGETABLES WALKED INTO THE LIBRARY?
... "PEAS WHISPER!"
YOE!
WHICH COUNTRY DO THEY SERVE IN THE SCHOOL CAFETERIA?
... CHILE!
WHICH OTHER COUNTRY DO THEY SERVE IN THE SCHOOL CAFETERIA?
... TURKEY!

HISTORY TEACHER: WHICH **PRESIDENT** WAS THE **ANGRIEST?**

SMART ALECK: MAD-ISON!

GARY: TEACHER, WHAT **COLOR** SHOULD I PAINT THE **CAT'S PICTURE?**

ART TEACHER: PURR-PLE!

WHAT **ORGANIZATION** DO **BRITISH PARENTS** BELONG TO?

... P-**TEA**-A!

TEACHER: WHERE WAS **ABRAHAM LINCOLN** BORN?

GEORGE: ILLINOIS!

TEACHER: WHICH **PART?**

GEORGE: ALL OF HIM!

POETRY CLASS

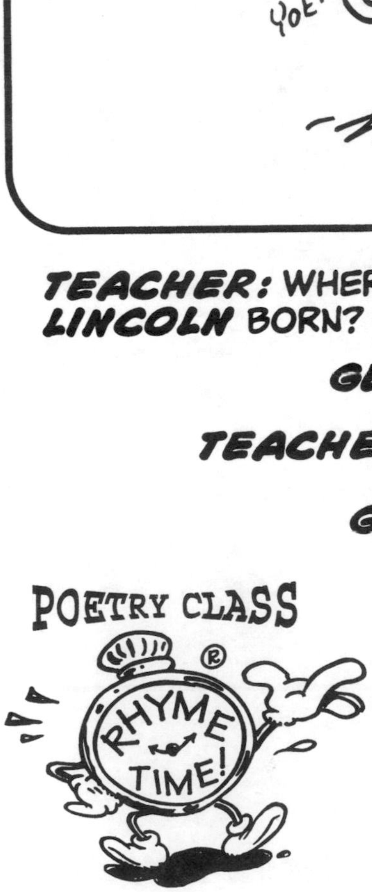

WHAT DO YOU CALL IT WHEN FRANKENSTEIN BECOMES A PROFESSOR?

A creature teacher!

TEACHER: HOW MUCH IS **5Q PLUS 5Q?**

PAUL: 10Q!

TEACHER: YOU'RE WELCOME!

WHAT HAS **FANGS** AND IS **WAITING FOR YOU AT 3:00?**

... AN **AFTER-SCHOOL SNAKE!**

AMY: THIS **WATER** IS **CLOUDY!**

LUNCH LADY: THE **WATER** IS **FINE.** THE **GLASS** IS JUST **DIRTY!**

TEACHER: I HOPE I **DIDN'T** JUST **SEE** YOU **CHEATING!**

TOM: I **HOPE** YOU **DIDN'T SEE** ME, **TOO!**

MAD ADD JOKE!

JACK-O-LANTERN
+ MATH FORMULA

PUMPKIN PI

GEOGRAPHY TEACHER: WHICH ***CITY*** HAS THE MOST ***BABY CHICKENS?***

SMART ALECK: CHICK-AGO!

WHAT DID THE ***OCEAN*** SAY WHEN ***SUMMER VACATION*** WAS OVER AND ***ALL*** THE ***KIDS*** WERE ***LEAVING?***

... NOTHING, IT JUST ***WAVED!***

COACH: WHICH IS ***BIGGER***, A ***FOOTBALL*** OR A ***BASEBALL?***

SMART ALECK: NEITHER! THEY ***BOTH*** HAVE ***EIGHT LETTERS!***

TERRY: Can I have more apple juice, please?

LUNCH LADY:* *Hey! Apples don't grow on trees!

WHAT DOES A ***SCHOOL JANITOR*** EAT AT THE ***MOVIES?***

... ***MOP***-CORN!

PATTY: HEY YOU'VE GOT YOUR ***THUMB*** ON MY ***HAMBURGER!***

LUNCH LADY: WELL, I DIDN'T WANT IT TO ***FALL*** ON THE ***FLOOR AGAIN!***

FIRST COACH: MY NEW **POLE VAULTER** CAN **JUMP HIGHER** THAN A **HOUSE!**

SECOND COACH: YEAH, BUT **HOUSES CAN'T JUMP!**

HOW DO YOU GET INTO THE **MUSIC APPRECIATION CLASS?**

... THROUGH THE **BACH** DOOR!

HISTORY TEACHER: WHAT WAS THE **GETTYSBURG ADDRESS?**

TOM: THE PLACE WHERE **GETTYSBURG LIVED!**

DID YOU HEAR THE JOKE ABOUT THE PENCIL?
... IT WAS POINTLESS!
YOE!
TEACHER: TOMMY, DO YOU HEAR SOMETHING?
TOMMY: NO.
TEACHER: THAT'S ODD, I'M TALKING TO YOU!
School Nurse Sick Jokes
PATTY: I HAVE A DRIPPY NOSE!
School Nurse: Does it run in your family?

KNOCK, KNOCK!
WHO'S THERE?
TENNESSEE!
TENNESSEE WHO?
TENNESSEE SUM OF ***5 + 5!***

JIM: I WANT TO BE A SUSPENSION ENGINEER WHEN I GROW UP!

School Counselor: Cross that bridge when you come to it!

SCHOOL NURSE: HAVE YOU EVER HAD THIS **BEFORE?**

ALICE: YES MA'AM.

SCHOOL NURSE: WELL, YOU'VE **GOT IT AGAIN!**

FANNY: MY TEACHER SAYS I'M **GREAT** AT **RECITING** THE **ALPHABET!**

GRANNY: TERRIFIC! WHAT COMES AFTER **A?**

FANNY: I DON'T KNOW. WE DIDN'T GET THAT **FAR** YET!

WHAT'S THE CHEAPEST SCHOOL SNACK?
... FREE-TOS!

TOM: NURSE, NURSE! I KEEP SEEING **STRIPED LEOPARDS!**

SCHOOL NURSE: HAVE YOU SEEN THE **SCHOOL PSYCHOLOGIST?**

TOM: NO, I JUST KEEP SEEING **STRIPED LEOPARDS!**

WHAT DOES A ***CHICKEN DRINK*** FOR AN ***AFTER-SCHOOL SNACK?***

... ***PEEP***-SI!

TEACHER: NAME ***FIVE THINGS*** THAT CONTAIN ***EGGS.***

SUE: OMELETS, CAKES, COOKIES AND ***TWO CHICKENS!***

SCIENCE TEACHER: WHAT DO **ANTS TAKE** WHEN THEY'RE **SICK?**

LARRY: ANT-IBIOTICS!

WHY DID THE **SCHOOL HIRE** A **TIGHTROPE WALKER** TO **WORK** IN THE **CAFETERIA?**

... SO THE **KIDS** WOULD HAVE A **BALANCED DIET!**

WHY DID THE SCHOOL JANITOR GET IN TROUBLE?
... HE WAS TALKIN' TRASH!

POETRY CLASS

RHYME TIME!

WHAT DO YOU CALL SOMEONE WHO HELPS YOU LEARN TO PLAY THE HORN?

A tooter tutor!

WHY COULDN'T THE ***PIANO TEACHER OPEN*** THE ***DOOR*** TO HIS ***CLASSROOM?***

... BECAUSE ALL THE ***KEYS*** WERE INSIDE!

WHY DID THE PIECE OF CORN JOIN THE SCHOOL BAND?
... IT HAD AN EAR FOR MUSIC!

WHY DID THE ***PAIR OF SCISSORS*** BECOME A ***SCHOOL BUS DRIVER?***

... IT KNEW A LOT OF SHORT ***CUTS!***

MAD® ADD JOKE!

PIG

+ LAUNDROMAT

HOGWASH

WHAT IS A ***SCHOOL LIBRARIAN'S*** FAVORITE ***FOOD?***

... MA-***SHHH***-ED POTATOES!

SCIENCE TEACHER: WHO CAN USE THE WORD ***"CLONE"*** IN A SENTENCE?

BOBBY: I WENT TO THE ***CIRCUS*** TO SEE ***THE CLONES!***

JON: THERE'S A ***LITTLE FLY*** IN THIS ***JELL-O!***

LUNCH LADY: OH, I'LL GET YOU A ***BIGGER*** ONE!

TEACHER: WILL YOU ***MAKE*** ME A ***CUP OF COFFEE?***

LUNCH LADY: ABRACADABRA – YOU'RE A ***CUP OF COFFEE!***

WHAT DID THE CAT SAY WHEN SHE GOT AN "F" ON HER MATH TEST?
... "NOBODY'S PURR-FECT!"

ROSIE: I'M ***HERE*** FOR ***MY THROAT!***

SCHOOL NURSE: I'M ***SORRY***, BUT I ***DON'T HAVE IT!***

WHAT DOES A ***DEER*** USE TO ***CARRY*** HER ***BOOKS?***

... A ***BUCK-PACK!***

DEBORAH: There's a dung beetle in my soup!

LUNCH LADY: Shh! Everyone will ask for one!

TEACHER: TOMMY, YOU'RE ***LATE*** FOR ***CLASS!***

TOMMY: NO, I'M ***EARLY*** FOR ***NEXT PERIOD!***

HISTORY TEACHER: WHICH **PRESIDENT** LOOKED LIKE A **VACUUM?**

SMART ALECK: HOOVER!

COUNSELOR CRACK UPS!

FRED: I WANT TO INSTALL MUFFLERS WHEN I GROW UP!

School Counselor: That's exhausting!

TEACHER: WHAT DO YOU GET IF YOU ***MULTIPLY 133,647 BY 43,012?***

BIFF: THE ***WRONG ANSWER!***

WHY IS A ***BOOK*** LIKE A ***WATERMELON?***

... BECAUSE ON THE ***INSIDE*** IT'S ***RED!***

IRA: I ***PLAY MUSIC*** BY ***EAR!***

MYRA: I ***LISTEN*** THE SAME WAY!

MY COUNTRY 'TIS OF THEE

WHICH **STATE** IS THE **SIMPLEST?**

AZ!

WHICH **STATE** IS THE MOST **JEALOUS?**

NV!

WHICH **STATE BREATHES** THE **MOST?**

AR!

WHICH **STATE TALKS** ON A **LOUDSPEAKER?**

PA!

WHICH **STATE** HAS THE **LEAST** IN IT?

MT!

WHICH ***STATE*** HAS THE MOST
DRIVER'S LICENSES?

ID!

HICH ***STATE WINS*** THE MOST
TV AWARDS?

ME!

WHICH ***STATE*** HAS THE MOST ***DOCTORS?***

MD!

WHICH ***STATE*** CAN YOU USE TO ***ROW A BOAT?***

OR!

HICH ***STATE*** DOESN'T HAVE AN ***OUTIE***
BELLY BUTTON?

NE!

HICH ***STATE*** IS THE
MOST ***AGREEABLE?***

OK!

MOM: HOW DO YOU LIKE YOUR **ASTRONOMY CLASS?**

TOM: IT'S LOOKING **UP!**

WAYNE: YOUR **THUMB** IS IN MY **SOUP!**

LUNCH LADY: DON'T **WORRY,** IT'S NOT THAT **HOT!**

MAD ADD JOKE!

FOOT
+ 18-WHEELER
TOE TRUCK

ENGLISH TEACHER: BOBBY, SPELL "***LADDER.***"

BOBBY: ***L-A-D-D-D-E-R.***

ENGLISH TEACHER: LEAVE ***OUT*** ONE OF THOSE "***D***"***S.***

BOBBY: WHICH ***ONE?***

WHAT DOES A HOME ECONOMICS TEACHER HAVE ON HER BED?
... A COOKIE SHEET!

WHAT DID THE ***SALT*** SAY WHEN IT MET THE ***PEPPER*** IN THE ***CAFETERIA?***

... "WHAT'S ***SHAKIN'?***"

STACEY: THERE'S A ***COCKROACH*** IN MY ***SOUP!***

LUNCH LADY: THERE'S PLENTY OF ***SOUP*** FOR YOU ***BOTH!***

TEACHER: WHAT KIND OF **ANIMALS** LIVE AT THE **NORTH POLE?**

TIMMY: COLD ONES!

WHY DID THE ROSE DO SO WELL IN SCHOOL?
... SHE WAS A BUDDING GENIUS!

GEOGRAPHY TEACHER: WHICH **CITY** HAS THE BEST **EYESIGHT?**

SMART ALECK: SEE-ATTLE!

LUNCH LADY: WHAT DO YOU **THINK** OF THE **BREAD?**

LULU: I **LOAF** IT!

PART I

BRIDGET: WHAT DO MOST **KITTENS** BECOME WHEN THEY **GROW UP?**

CLASS CLOWN: CAT-ERERS!

GEORGE: HOW DID **GOLDILOCKS** FIND AN **EMPTY HOUSE?**

CLASS CLOWN: BEAR LEFT!

LOU: DID YOU **HEAR** THAT **HUMPTY DUMPTY** HAD A **GREAT FALL?**

CLASS CLOWN: YEAH – IT WAS MUCH **BETTER** THAN HIS **SUMMER!**

CAROL: WHO IS THE MOST **TRUSTWORTHY** PERSON IN AN **OFFICE?**

CLASS CLOWN: SECRET-ARIES!

JOANNE: WHICH **TYPE** OF **CANDY** IS THE **LOUDEST?**

CLASS CLOWN: YELL-Y BEANS!

LUKE: I CAN **PLAY ANYTHING** ON MY **GUITAR!**

CLASS CLOWN: OK! **PLAY** THE **TROMBONE** ON IT!

WILBUR: HOW **FAR** CAN YOU **WALK** IN THE **FOREST?**

CLASS CLOWN: HALF WAY. THEN YOU'LL BE **WALKING OUT!**

STAN: HOW MUCH IS A SODA?

LUNCH LADY: ONE DOLLAR.

STAN: HOW MUCH IS A REFILL?

LUNCH LADY: FREE.

STAN: I'LL HAVE ONE REFILL, PLEASE.

POETRY CLASS

WHERE DO YOU FIND THE KEYS TO OPEN THE SCHOOL CLINIC?

A nurse purse!

TOM: THIS ***SONG*** I'M SINGING IS ***HARD!***

MUSIC TEACHER: I WISH IT WERE ***IMPOSSIBLE!***

WHY DID THE STUDENT DROP HIS COMPUTER CLASS?
... HE WAS KEY-BORED!

WHY DID THE ***DUCK*** GET SENT TO THE ***PRINCIPAL'S OFFICE?***

... HE KEPT MAKING ***WISE QUACKS!***

ON WHAT DAY DO THEY SERVE FISH IN THE CAFETERIA?
... FRY-DAY!

SARA: WHAT SHOULD I WEAR TO THE **DANCE** WITH MY NEW ***PURPLE-AND-ORANGE POLKA DOT SOCKS?***

DAD: A PAIR OF ***TALL BOOTS!***

TEACHER: MURRAY, THIS **HOMEWORK** IS IN YOUR ***BROTHER'S HANDWRITING!***

MURRAY: THAT'S BECAUSE I ***BORROWED*** HIS ***PENCIL!***

LAURA: MY AUNT SWALLOWED POISON!

School Nurse: Give her this auntie-dote!

TEDDY: THERE'S A **COCKROACH** IN MY **SOUP!**

LUNCH LADY: I DIDN'T KNOW YOU WERE A **VEGETARIAN!**

WHICH ANIMAL IS FOUND IN THE ALPHABET?
... EWE!

WHICH **TWO ANIMALS** ARE FOUND IN THE **ALPHABET?**

... DOUBLE **EWE!**

TEACHER: DONNY, IF YOU DON'T STOP **ACTING UP** I'M GOING TO **CALL** YOUR MOTHER **IMMEDIATELY!**

DONNY: WHY WOULD YOU **CALL** HER **IMMEDIATELY?** HER **NAME** IS **RITA!**

WHAT DID THE ***SORE BACK*** GET ON ITS ***REPORT CARD?***

... STRAIGHT ***ACHES!***

LISA: This food isn't fit for a dog!

LUNCH LADY: Hold on, I'll get some that is!

DEAN: WHAT DID YOU THINK OF THE ***QUESTIONS ON THE QUIZ?***

JEAN: THE ***QUESTIONS*** WERE FINE. THE ***ANSWERS*** WERE THE ***HARD PART!***

WHAT KIND OF ***DOG*** DOES A ***SCIENCE TEACHER*** HAVE?

... A YELLOW ***LAB!***

WHY DID THE STUDENT FAIL DRIVER'S ED?
... HE TOOK A CRASH COURSE!

MATH TEACHER: IF I HAD ***TEN BASEBALLS IN ONE HAND*** AND ***TWELVE IN THE OTHER,*** WHAT WOULD I HAVE?

EDDIE: REALLY ***HUGE HANDS!***

GEOGRAPHY

HEE HEE!

GEOGRAPHY TEACHER: WHAT IS A **PAIR OF EYEGLASSES'** FAVORITE **STATE?**

SMART ALECK: EYE-DAHO!

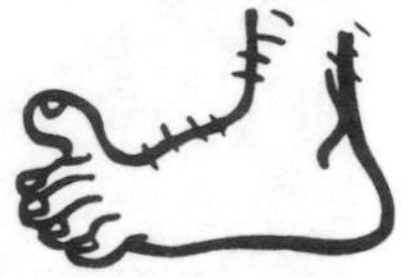

GEOGRAPHY TEACHER: WHICH **STATE** IS THE **FRIENDLIEST?**

SMART ALECK: O-**HI**-O!

GEOGRAPHY TEACHER: WHICH **STATE** GOES TO THE **DOCTOR A LOT?**

SMART ALECK: ILL-INOIS!

GEOGRAPHY TEACHER: WHICH **STATE** HAS THE MOST **SCISSORS?**

SMART ALECK: CONNECTI-**CUT!**

GEOGRAPHY TEACHER: WHICH **STATE** IS **NO LONGER PART** OF THE **UNITED STATES?**

SMART ALECK: ORE-**GONE!**

LUNCH LADY: WE'RE NOT GOING TO ***SERVE SAUSAGES*** ANY ***LONGER.***

PRINCIPAL: WHY NOT?

LUNCH LADY: BECAUSE THEY'RE ALREADY ***LONG ENOUGH!***

WHAT SHOULD YOU DO WHEN THE CAFETERIA SERVES BLUEBERRIES?
... TRY TO CHEER THEM UP!

WHO IS THE ***MOST ATHLETIC BOY IN SCHOOL?***

... JIM!

NATALIE: I KEEP SEEING ***IMAGINARY SHEEP!***

SCHOOL NURSE: THAT'S ***BAAAAD!***

GEOGRAPHY TEACHER: WHO CAN TELL ME WHERE ***FRANCE*** IS?

PIERRE: ON ***PAGE 34!***

COUNSELOR CRACK UPS!

BEN: I WANT TO BE A BASKETBALL PLAYER WHEN I GROW UP!

School Counselor: You'll have a ball!

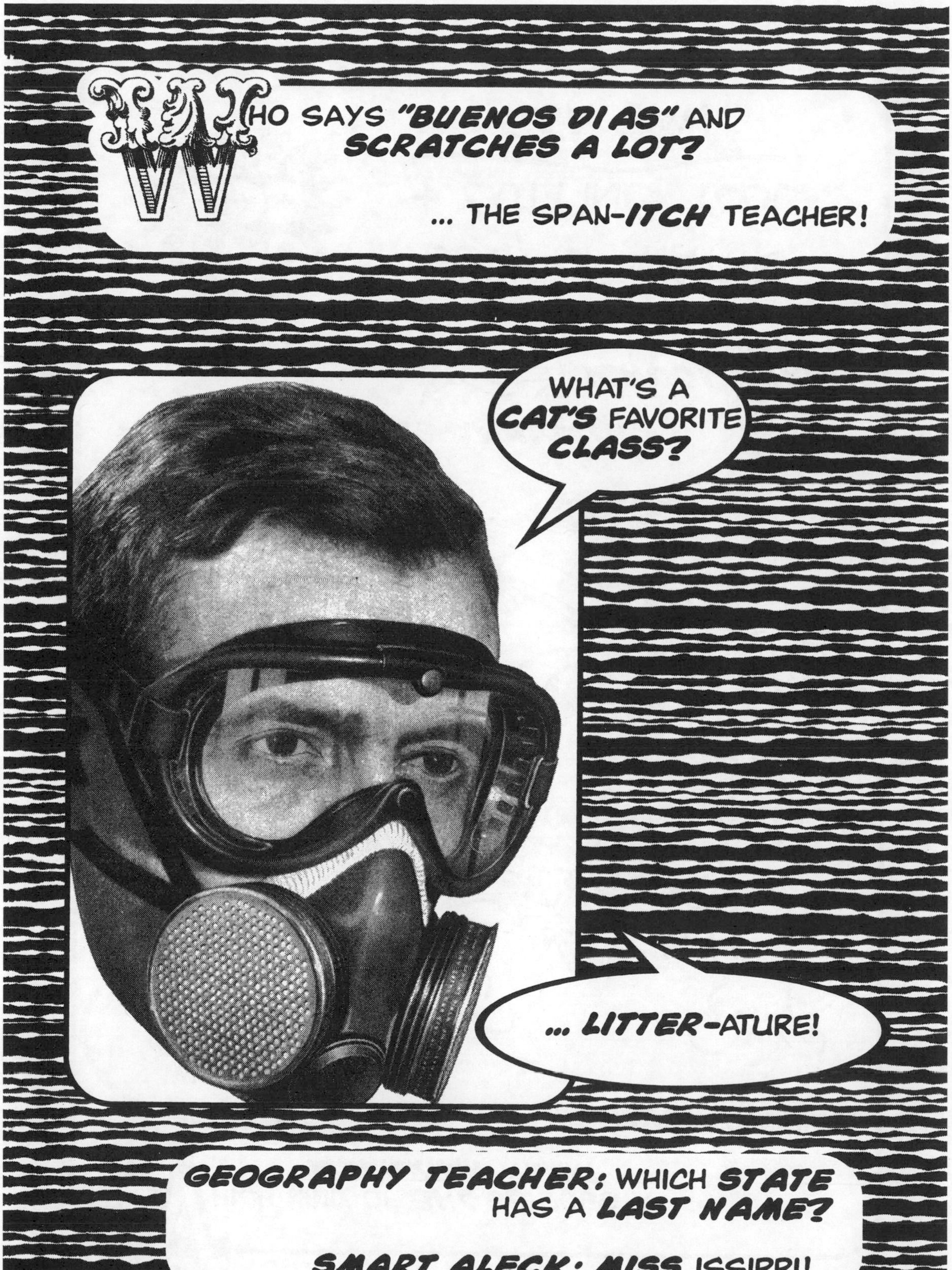
WHO SAYS "BUENOS DIAS" AND SCRATCHES A LOT?
... THE SPAN-ITCH TEACHER!
WHAT'S A CAT'S FAVORITE CLASS?
... LITTER-ATURE!
GEOGRAPHY TEACHER: WHICH STATE HAS A LAST NAME?
SMART ALECK: MISS ISSIPPI!

WHICH KIND OF ***SHOES*** DOES A ***LIBRARIAN*** WEAR?

... ***HUSH*** PUPPIES!

TODD: I THINK I HAVE ***AMNESIA!***

SCHOOL NURSE: ***FORGET*** IT!

MAD ADD JOKE!

BODY OF WATER
+ CUTTING TOOL

SEA SAW

WHAT DID THE ***BOY SNAKE*** GIVE TO THE ***GIRL SNAKE*** AT THE END OF THE ***SCHOOL DANCE?***

... A GOOD-NIGHT ***HISS!***

KNOCK-KNOCK?
... WHO'S THERE?
STU!
... STU WHO?
STU-DENT BODY!

HOW DO YOU GET FROM JUNIOR HIGH SCHOOL TO HIGH SCHOOL? ... USE A LADDER!
HISTORY TEACHER: WHICH PRESIDENT LOOKED LIKE A CAR?
SMART ALECK: FORD!
TIM: I HAVE A TEST ON MARK TWAIN TODAY!
JIM: LOTS OF HUCK!

WHERE DO ***BABY TREES*** GO TO ***SCHOOL?***

... A NURSERY!

KRISTEN: IF I MAKE THE ***CHEERLEADING SQUAD***, I'LL ***YELL!***

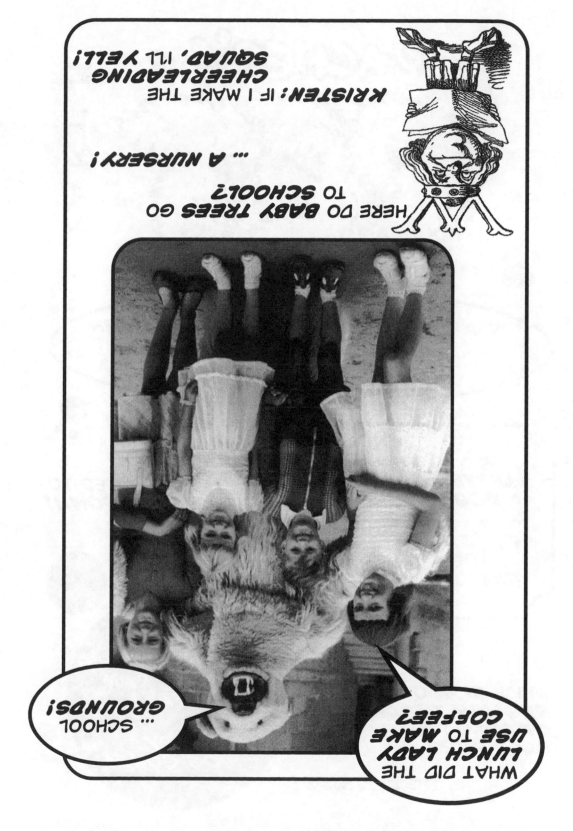

TEACHER'S PET PART II

WHAT DOES THE ***LUNCH LADY'S KITTEN*** LIKE ON HER ***HOT DOG?***

... ***CAT-***SUP!

WHY DID THE ***MUSIC TEACHER*** GET A ***PET DUCK?***

... HE WANTED TO ***GET DOWN!***

WHY IS THE ***LETTER G*** LIKE A ***DOG'S TAIL?***

... IT'S AT THE ***END*** OF A ***DOG!***

MARY: THE ENGLISH TEACHER'S ***PUPPY RAN AWAY!***

GARY: DOG-GONE!

WHICH ***SIDE*** OF THE ***ENGLISH TEACHER'S CAT*** HAS THE MOST ***FUR?***

... THE ***OUTSIDE!***

WHAT DO YOU GET IF YOU ***CROSS A CAT WITH A DOG?***

... AN ANIMAL THAT ***FIGHTS*** WITH ITSELF!

NED: MY DOG HAS LOTS OF ***FLEAS!***

TED: HOW MUCH IS THAT IN ***DOG YEARS?***

WHERE DOES THE ***FRENCH TEACHER*** GET PET SUPPLIES FOR HER ***KITTEN?***

... FROM A ***CAT***-ALOG!

PEG: DID YOU HEAR THAT THE ***ART TEACHER'S CAT*** IS ***CRABBY?***

MEG: YEAH, IT'S A ***SOUR-PUSS!***

WHY IS THE ***WORLD HISTORY TEACHER SAD*** ABOUT HER ***FROG?***

... HE ***CROAKED!***

RICHIE: I JUST ***SAT*** ON A ***THUMBTACK!***

SCHOOL NURSE: WHAT'S THE ***POINT?***

WHAT DO YOU CALL A FISH THAT GOES TO SCHOOL?

A class bass!

ENGLISH TEACHER:* A, B, C, D, E, F, G, H, I, J...WHAT COMES AFTER *J?

JESSICA: WALKING!

WHERE DID THE ***QUEEN BEE*** GO TO ***SCHOOL?***

... ***BUZZ***-INESS SCHOOL!

ANNE: IF I MAKE THE ***SWIM TEAM,*** I'LL MAKE A ***BIG SPLASH!***

PHIL: I FEEL ***RUN DOWN!***

SCHOOL NURSE: DID YOU GET THE ***NUMBER*** OF THE ***LICENSE PLATE?***

WHICH LETTER IS ALWAYS ASKING QUESTIONS?

Y!

WHAT IS A ***WAITER'S*** FAVORITE PART OF A ***SCHOOL BASKETBALL GAME?***
... THE ***TIP***-OFF!
Pompeian.

BILL: I'M GOING TO ***TRY OUT*** FOR THE ***SCHOOL HOCKEY TEAM!***

JILL: GOOD PUCK!

WHAT ***SPORT*** DOES THE ***MATH TEACHER*** LIKE?

... ***FIGURE*** SKATING!

TEACHER: YOU REALLY NEED TO LEARN ***DECIMALS!***

TOM: WHAT'S THE ***POINT?***

GEOGRAPHY TEACHER: WHICH **STATE** IS **WARMEST** IN **WINTER?**

SMART ALECK: SOUTH DA-**COAT**-A!

CLIZIA: HELP ME, I THINK I'M INVISIBLE!

School Nurse: Sorry, I can't see you now!

ENGLISH TEACHER: HOW MANY ***LETTERS*** ARE THERE IN ***THE ALPHABET?***

BO: ELEVEN! T-H-E-A-L-P-H-A-B-E-T!

WHICH KIND OF TESTS WOULD YOU GET IF A CHICKEN WAS YOUR TEACHER?
... EGGS-AMS!

WHAT DOES A ***BASEBALL COACH*** KEEP ON HIS ***DOORSTEP?***

... A ***MITT!***

GEOGRAPHY TEACHER: WHERE IS ***NEVADA?***

BEKAH: I DON'T HAVE THE ***VEGAS*** IDEA!

LARRY: TEACHER, I DON'T HAVE MY ***HOMEWORK*** BECAUSE A ***TEN-FOOT TALL LION ATE IT!***

TEACHER: THAT'S SOME ***LYIN'!***

WHY DID THE ***PENCIL*** GO TO THE ***SCHOOL NURSE?***
... IT HAD ***LEAD***-LICE!

WHY DID THE ***STUDENT*** STOP EATING ***PIZZAS?***

... HIS ***HEALTH TEACHER*** TOLD HIM HE NEEDS TO EAT ***SQUARE MEALS!***

WHAT DOES A **SNOWMAN EAT** WHEN THE **CAFETERIA** SERVES **MEXICAN FOOD?**

... **BRR**-ITOS!

HECTOR: I THINK I'M A **PARAKEET!**

SCHOOL NURSE: I CAN'T **TWEET** THAT!

MAD ADD JOKE!

GHOST
+ SOMETHING YOU CHEW

BOO-BLE GUM

WHAT DO YOU NEED TO ***TAKE*** TO GET INTO ***DENTAL SCHOOL?***

... AN ***ORAL*** EXAM!

MAD ADD JOKE!

MONEY
+ SCRAM

CASH-SHOO!

GEOGRAPHY TEACHER: WHICH ***STATE*** IS THE MOST ***CURIOUS?***

SMART ALECK: HA-***WHY***-II!

WILLY: I KEEP THINKING WE HAVE A ***TEST TODAY!***

LILLY: WE ***DO*** HAVE A ***TEST TODAY!***

WILLY: I KNOW. THAT'S WHY I KEEP ***THINKING*** IT!

WHAT KIND OF ***ICE CREAM*** DID THE ***SNAKE*** ORDER IN THE ***SCHOOL CAFETERIA?***

... ***ASP***-BERRY!

GEOGRAPHY TEACHER: WHICH ***CITY*** IS REALLY ***ODD?***

SMART ALECK: ALBU-***QUIRKY!***

KNOCK, KNOCK?
...WHO'S THERE?
JUSTIN!
... JUSTIN WHO?
JUSTIN TIME FOR ***MATH CLASS!***

COUNSELOR CRACK UPS!

CLEO: I THINK I CAN SEE THE FUTURE!

School Counselor:
Since when?!

CLEO: NEXT TUESDAY!

PHOTOGRAPHY TEACHER: I ***SWALLOWED*** A ***ROLL OF FILM!***

SCHOOL NURSE: SEE WHAT ***DEVELOPS!***

WHAT DOES A ***WATCH EAT*** WHEN THE ***CAFETERIA*** SERVES ***MEXICAN FOOD?***

... TICK TACOS!

WILL: This beef stew tastes like old socks!

LUNCH LADY: Oops! I must have given you the wrong dish. The beef stew tastes like pond scum!

WHY DIDN'T THE **NOSE** MAKE THE **SCHOOL BASKETBALL TEAM?**
... HE DIDN'T GET **PICKED!**

TEACHER: JOY, ARE YOU **SLEEPING** IN **CLASS?**

JOY: NO **MA'AM!** I'M **WATCHING MOVIES** ON THE **BACK OF MY EYELIDS!**

PATTY: I HAVE A **BAD COUGH!**

SCHOOL NURSE: GO TO THE **ENGLISH TEACHER** AND **STICK** OUT YOUR **TONGUE!**

PATTY: HOW'S **THAT** GOING TO **HELP?**

SCHOOL NURSE: IT **WON'T,** BUT **I DON'T LIKE** THE **ENGLISH TEACHER!**

WHICH **STATE** DID THE **GEOGRAPHY TEACHER** SAY IS THE **BEST DANCER?**

... **KAN-KAN**SAS!

WHAT DOES A MUSIC TEACHER PLAY ON AN ELECTRIC GUITAR?
... ELECTRIC CORDS!

TEACHER: WHY ARE YOU SO **TIRED** TODAY?

BRIAN: MY **BROTHER** THINKS HE'S A **REFRIGERATOR!**

TEACHER: SO WHY DOES THAT MAKE **YOU TIRED?**

BRIAN: BECAUSE HE SLEEPS WITH HIS **MOUTH OPEN** AND THAT **LITTLE LIGHT** KEEPS ME **AWAKE ALL NIGHT!**

Klass Full of Kates

WHICH ***KATE*** IS THE ***SHORTEST?***

... LO-KATE!

WHICH ***KATE LOVES SCHOOL?***

... EDU-KATE!

WHICH ***KATE*** IS A ***CLONE?***

... DUPLI-KATE!

WHICH ***KATE*** IS ALWAYS ***ABSENT?***

... VA-KATE!

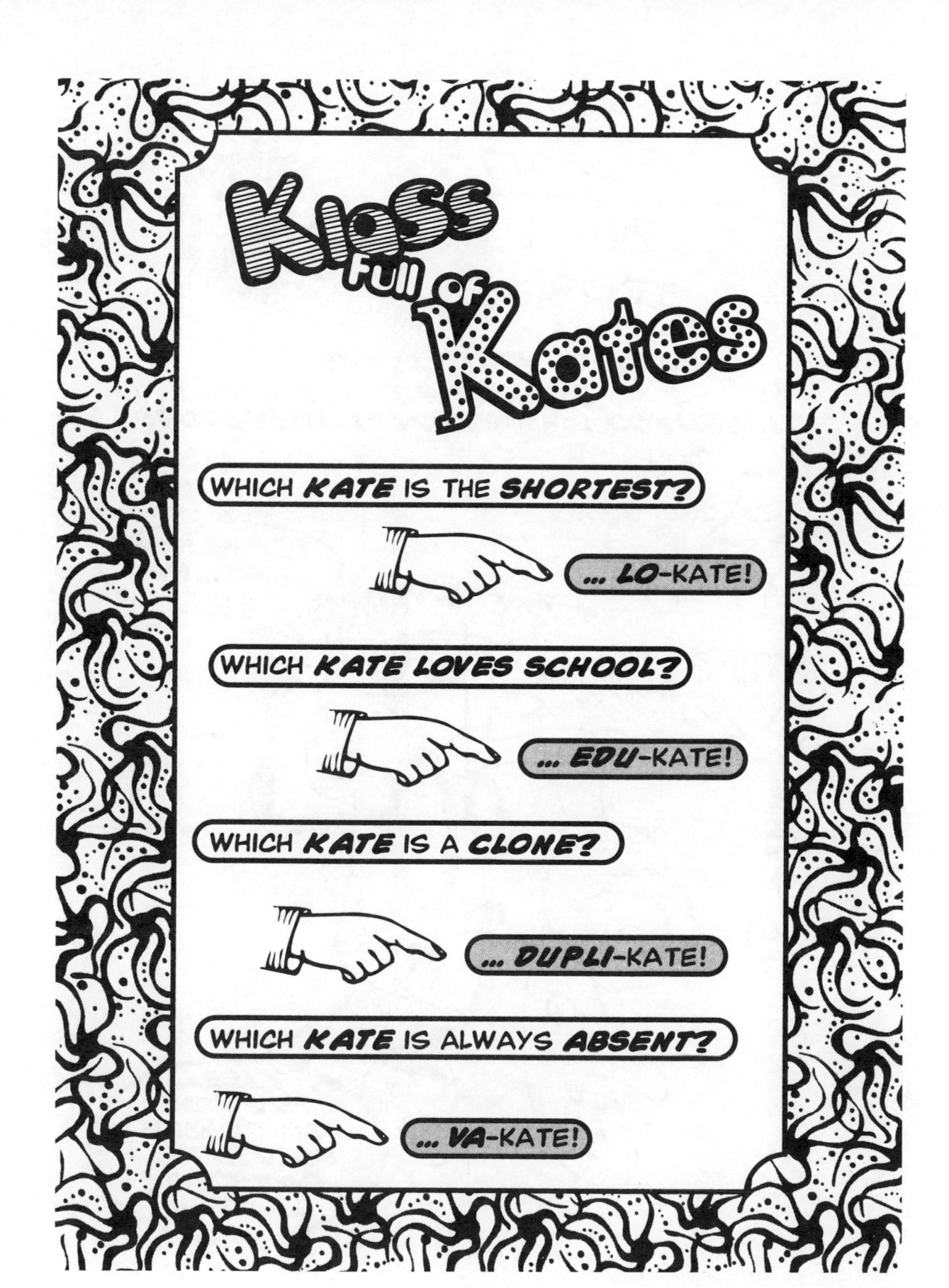

GEOGRAPHY TEACHER: WHAT **CONTINENT** CAN YOU USE TO **TOW THINGS?**

SMART ALECK: EU-**ROPE!**

MAD® ADD JOKE!

PRISONER
+ QUIZ
———
CON-TEST

WHO IS THE ***SLOPPIEST PERSON*** AT A ***SCHOOL PEP RALLY?***

... THE ***MESS-COT!***

WHY DID THE TONGUE STAY UP LATE?
... BECAUSE IT WAS CRAMMING FOR ITS TASTE TEST!

WHY DID THE ***SHOELACE*** GET SENT TO THE ***PRINCIPAL'S OFFICE?***

... IT WAS ACTING ***KNOTTY!***

KNOCK, KNOCK!
... WHO'S THERE?
ALEXA!
... ALEXA WHO?
ALEXA ONE MORE TIME FOR YOUR ***HOMEWORK,*** THEN YOU'RE GOING TO THE ***PRINCIPAL'S OFFICE!***

WHAT KIND OF **TEST** DOES A **CHEERLEADER** TAKE?

... A **PEP QUIZ!**

MATTHEW: MOM, CAN YOU **WRITE** YOUR **NAME** WITH YOUR **EYELIDS CLOSED?**

MOM: YEAH, **PROBABLY.**

MATTHEW: TERRIFIC! CAN YOU **CLOSE** YOUR **EYES** AND **SIGN** MY **REPORT CARD?**

WHAT DID THE ***MUSIC TEACHER*** PUT ON HER ***PAPER CUT?***

... BACH-TINE!

ANDREA: MY ***HEAD*** FEELS ***FUNNY!***

SCHOOL NURSE: SO DON'T ***TOUCH*** IT!

SCHOOL NURSE: AND WHY DON'T YOU THINK YOU CAN TAKE THE MATH TEST TODAY?

Donovan: I have ar–itch–matic!

SHOP TEACHER: WE'RE GOING TO ***LEARN*** TO ***DRILL*** TODAY IN ***SHOP CLASS!***

LOU: THAT SOUNDS ***BORE***-ING!

COUNSELOR CRACK UPS!

BRUNO: I WANT TO BE A FARMER WHEN I GROW UP!

School Counselor: That's a growing field!

SCIENCE TEACHER: WHAT DO YOU ***CALL*** THE ***HAIR*** ON A ***GIRAFFE'S TAIL?***

KAREN: GIRAFFE HAIR!

WHY DID THE ARTIST DO SO WELL ON HIS TEST?
... HE HAD A STROKE OF GENIUS!

HOW DOES A ***CHEERLEADER CONNECT*** TO THE ***INTERNET?***

... SHE USES ***A-O-YELL!***

NANCY: YOU HAVE TO ***CURE*** MY ***RUNNY NOSE*** NOW!

SCHOOL NURSE: DON'T GET ***SNOTTY*** WITH ME!

SARA: WHEN I **WAKE UP** IN THE **MORNING,** MY **HEAD HURTS** FOR AN **HOUR.**

SCHOOL NURSE: TRY **WAKING UP** AN HOUR **LATER!**

WHICH **STATE** DID THE **GEOGRAPHY TEACHER** SAY IS THE **TINIEST?**

... **MINI**-SOTA!

BRITANY: I KEEP SEEING **DOUBLE!**

SCHOOL NURSE: HAVE A **SEAT.**

BRITANY: WHICH **ONE?**

MAD® ADD JOKE!

PORCUPINE
+ BALLOON
———
POP

BRAD: COACH, THESE **NEW SNEAKERS HURT!**

COACH: YOU'VE GOT THEM ON THE **WRONG FEET!**

BRAD: THESE ARE THE ONLY **FEET** I **HAVE!**

HOWARD: HOW CAN YOU TELL IF **DESSERT** WAS REALLY **DELICIOUS?**

CLASS CLOWN: YOU'LL GET TWO **YUMS** UP!

MICKEY: WHAT DO YOU CALL **SOMEONE** WHO WEARS A **UNIFORM** AND **HELPS OLD LADIES CROSS** THE **OCEAN?**

CLASS CLOWN: A **BUOY** SCOUT!

MATTHEW: WHY CAN'T A **SNAKE RIDE** A **BICYCLE?**

CLASS CLOWN: IT DOESN'T HAVE A **THUMB** TO **RING** THE **BELL!**

ALICE: WHAT'S THE **HARDEST PART** ABOUT **PARACHUTING?**

CLASS CLOWN: THE **GROUND!**

ALEX: WHAT'S THE BEST **BOAT** TO **SIT** ON?

CLASS CLOWN: A **BUTT**-LE SHIP!

EDDIE: WHAT IS A **PEN'S** FAVORITE **DRINK?**

CLASS CLOWN: INK LEMONADE!

ROSE: WHY DO **CIRCUS PERFORMERS** LOVE **CAMPING?**

CLASS CLOWN: THEY ALWAYS HAVE THE **BIGGEST TENT!**

GYM TEACHER: TODAY WE'RE GOING TO LEARN **FENCING!**

ANNA: WHAT'S THE **POINT?**

HOW DID THE PIG WIN THE SCHOOL BASEBALL GAME?
... HE HIT A GRAND HAM!

KNOCK, KNOCK?
...WHO'S THERE?
HARLEY!
... HARLEY WHO?
HARLEY HEAR YA TEACHER, CAN YOU **SPEAK UP?**

MARTHA: There's a fly in my soup!

LUNCH LADY: ***Don't worry, I'm not charging you extra!***

MARY: I HEARD YOU HAVE TO GO TO ***COURT!***

GARY: YEAH, I'M TAKING A ***TENNIS CLASS!***

ALAN: I THINK I HAVE THE ***MEASLES!***

SCHOOL NURSE: THAT'S A ***RASH*** STATEMENT!

GEOGRAPHY TEACHER: WHICH ***STATE*** HAS THE ***BIGGEST PHONE BILL?***

SMART ALECK: CALL-IFORNIA!

SCHOOL NURSE: WHERE DID YOU GET THIS **STING** FROM?

JOY: IN **THIRD PERIOD** WE HAD A **SPELLING BEE!**

WHY DID THE ALIEN DO SO WELL IN SCHOOL?
... HIS GRADES WERE OUT OF THIS WORLD!
YOE!

GEOGRAPHY TEACHER: WHAT **CONTINENT** HAS THE MOST **INSECTS?**

SMART ALECK: ANT-ARCTICA!

WHAT IS YOUR EXCUSE WHEN YOU GET AN "F" ON YOUR REPORT CARD?

A fail tale!

IF I MAKE the TEAM!

STELLA: IF I MAKE THE ***TUMBLING TEAM,*** I'M GONNA ***FLIP!***

SARA: IF I MAKE THE ***BASKETBALL TEAM,*** I'M GONNA HAVE A ***BALL!***

TOM: IF I MAKE THE ***BASEBALL TEAM,*** I'M GONNA GO ***BATTY!***

ADRIAN: IF I MAKE THE ***SOCCER TEAM,*** IT'S GONNA BE A REAL ***KICK!***

ETHAN: IF I MAKE THE ***DEBATE TEAM,*** I'LL BE ***SPEECHLESS!***

TAD: IF I MAKE THE ***TRACK TEAM,*** I'LL HAVE OVERCOME A ***BIG HURDLE!***

KATHY: IF I MAKE THE ***SOCCER TEAM,*** I'LL HAVE ACHIEVED MY ***GOALS!***

DANIELLE: IF I MAKE THE ***TENNIS TEAM,*** I'LL RAISE A ***RACKET!***

ERIC: IF I MAKE THE ***HOCKEY TEAM,*** I'LL ***STICK*** TO IT!

DONNA: IF I MAKE THE ***SKATING TEAM,*** THAT WOULD BE ***ICE!***

BILL: IF I MAKE THE ***GOLF TEAM,*** THAT WOULD BE A ***HOLE*** LOT OF FUN!

ANDREW: IF I MAKE THE ***BOWLING TEAM,*** I'LL HAVE NO TIME TO ***SPARE!***

JASON: IF I MAKE THE ***FOOTBALL TEAM,*** I'LL HAVE TO ***PASS!***

LYNN: IF I MAKE THE ***VOLLEYBALL TEAM,*** I'LL ***JUMP*** FOR JOY!

WHAT DO YOU CALL **SOMEONE** WHO'S **GOOD** AT **GEOMETRY** AND **SPORTS?**

... A **MATHLETE!**

WHY DID THE PODIATRIST GET KICKED OUT OF THE SCHOOL CAFETERIA?
... HE DIDN'T HAVE ENOUGH MONEY TO FOOT THE BILL!

SAM: DAD, WILL YOU DO MY **MATH HOMEWORK?**

DAD: NO, THAT WOULD BE **WRONG.**

SAM: OH, THAT'S RIGHT, YOU'RE NOT **GOOD AT MATH.** I'LL ASK **MOM.**

MAD® ADD JOKE!

14 KARATS
+ FLOUNDER
GOLDFISH

GEOGRAPHY TEACHER: WHAT ***CONTINENT*** IS ALWAYS ***BEHIND?***

SMART ALECK: AUS-***TRAIL***-IA!

TAKING ATTENDANCE

TEACHER: **JOHN BARBER!**

JOHN BARBER: **HAIR!**

TEACHER: **BILLY RABBIT!**

BILLY RABBIT: **HARE!**

TEACHER: **LARRY LAUGH!**

LARRY LAUGH: **HAR!**

TEACHER: **FRANK N. STEIN!**

FRANK N. STEIN: **HORROR!**

TEACHER: **E. R. LOBE!**

E. R. LOBE: **HEAR!**

TEACHER: **EM PLOYER!**

EM PLOYER: **HIRE!**

WHY DID THE ***GIRL*** BRING ***SCISSORS*** TO ***SCHOOL?***

... SHE WANTED TO ***CUT*** IN THE ***LUNCH LINE!***

ENGLISH TEACHER: WHAT WAS ***HAMLET'S SON'S NAME?***

OLIVIA: PIGLET!

WHAT'S THE ***SCHOOL COLOR*** FOR A SCHOOL WITH ***GOOD ENGLISH STUDENTS?***

... RED!

WHY DID THE GOAT GET KICKED OUT OF CLASS?
... HE WAS KIDDING AROUND!
GLÜCK AUF!

GEOGRAPHY TEACHER: GREG, NAME AN ***ANIMAL*** THAT ***LIVES IN AUSTRALIA.***

GREG: A ***KANGAROO!***

GEOGRAPHY TEACHER: GOOD. NOW ***NAME ANOTHER.***

GREG: ANOTHER KANGAROO!

WHAT IS THE ***HISTORY TEACHER'S*** NAME?

... CYBILL WARR!

WHICH STATE IS A FOOTBALL PLAYER'S FAVORITE?
... NEW JERSEY!
YOE!

SIGN IN THE ***SHOWER*** IN THE ***GYM LOCKER ROOM:***

WE'RE ***NEVER CLOTHED!***

MAD ADD JOKE!

SURFER
+ FARM
DUDE RANCH

WHAT IS A FOX'S FAVORITE SUBJECT?
... SLY-ENCE CLASS!
WHY DID THE BOY RIDE HIS BIKE TO SCHOOL?
... BECAUSE IT WAS TOO HEAVY TO CARRY!
FIRST PIG: OINK!
SECOND PIG: MOOO-OO!
FIRST PIG: WHAT DO YOU MEAN "MOOO-OO!"?
SECOND PIG: TO GRADUATE I HAVE TO LEARN A FOREIGN LANGUAGE!

HISTORY TEACHER: WHEN WAS **ABRAHAM LINCOLN BORN?**

NICKY: ON **LINCOLN'S BIRTHDAY!**

WHAT DID THE **HAND** DO AFTER IT **GRADUATED** FROM **HIGH SCHOOL?**
... IT JOINED THE **ARM**-Y!

SCHOOL NURSE: HAVE YOU EVER HAD ANY **PROBLEMS** BEFORE WITH **ECZEMA?**

HALLIE: ONLY IN **SPELLING CLASS!**

TEACHER: IS THIS YOUR **PAPER?** THE **NAME** IS **SMUDGED!**

JOHNNY: NO, MY NAME'S NOT **SMUDGED.** IT'S **JOHNNY.**

WHAT DID THE ICE-CREAM CONE GET AT GRADUATION?
... A DIP-LOMA!

KNOCK-KNOCK?
... WHO'S THERE?
RHODA!
... RHODA WHO?
RHODA THE **BUS** TO **SCHOOL** TODAY!

WHAT DOES THE **TEACHER'S KITTEN** LIKE TO **WATCH ON TV?**

... CAT-TOONS!

SCIENCE TEACHER: WHAT KIND OF **ANT** IS **GRAY?**

LUKE: AN ELEPH-**ANT!**

WHAT DO YOU CALL THE STICK THAT THE TEACHER'S DOG RAN THREE BLOCKS TO GET?
... FAR-FETCHED!

MAD ADD JOKE!

GOLFER
\+ ACTORS
FORE-CAST

SHARON: I'M GOING TO JOIN THE **ASTRONOMY CLUB** AND **HANG OUT WITH STARS!**

HARVEY: I GOT A **RASH** FROM **BITING MOSQUITOS!**

SCHOOL NURSE: WELL, STOP **BITING MOSQUITOS!**

WHICH STATE DID THE GEOGRAPHY TEACHER SAY HAS THE MOST ANIMALS?
... FUR-MONT!
YOE!

NANCY: TEACHER, EXCUSE ME FOR BEING **LATE** TODAY. THE **SNOW** WAS REALLY **DEEP!**

TEACHER: THAT'S OK, I GET YOUR **DRIFT!**

Kelly: There's a moth on my ham!

LUNCH LADY: Don't worry, the spider on your lettuce will eat it!

GEOGRAPHY TEACHER: WHAT IS A SHEEP'S FAVORITE STATE?
SMART ALECK: EWE-TAH!
WHAT HAPPENED WHEN THE MATH TEACHER TRIPPED AND FELL?
... HE FRACTIONED HIS ARM!
MATH TEACHER: WHICH NUMBER IS THE BEST GOLFER?
SMART ALECK: 4!
SCIENCE TEACHER: WHAT DO YOU CALL AN ELEPHANT WITH CURLY HAIR?
LIZ: A PACHY-PERM!

WHICH ***STATE*** DID THE ***GEOGRAPHY TEACHER*** SAY YOU GO TO WHEN YOU GET ***SENT*** TO ***PRISON?***

... ***CON***-NECTICUT!

WHY DID THE PRINCIPAL CROSS THE ROAD?
... BECAUSE IT WAS THE CHICKEN'S DAY OFF!

SCHOOL SECRETARY: THERE ARE SOME ***PARENTS*** HERE TO ***SEE*** YOU.

PRINCIPAL: TELL THEM I'M ***NOT HERE.***

SCHOOL SECRETARY: I DID, BUT THEY ***WOULDN'T BELIEVE*** ME!

PRINCIPAL: OK, THEN ***I'LL*** GO ***TELL*** THEM!

GEOGRAPHY TEACHER: WHAT IS A **LION'S** FAVORITE **STATE?**

SMART ALECK: MANE!

GEOGRAPHY TEACHER: WHICH **STATE** MAKES THE MOST **SANDWICHES?**

SMART ALECK: DELI-WARE!

GEOGRAPHY TEACHER: WHICH **STATE** IS THE **LOUDEST?**

SMART ALECK: ILLI-**NOISE!**

GEOGRAPHY TEACHER: WHICH IS A **TRAIN'S** FAVORITE **STATE?**

SMART ALECK: MASSA-**CHOO-CHOO**-SETTS!

GEOGRAPHY TEACHER: WHICH **STATE** USES THE MOST **STRAWS?**

SMART ALECK: MINNE-**SODA!**

GEOGRAPHY TEACHER: WHICH **CITY** WANDERS AROUND **AIMLESSLY?**

SMART ALECK: ROME!

WHAT DOES A RADIATOR EAT WHEN THE SCHOOL CAFETERIA SERVES MEXICAN FOOD?
... FA-HEAT-AS!
SCIENCE TEACHER: WHY DO HUMMINGBIRDS HUM?
REBECCA: BECAUSE THEY DON'T KNOW THE WORDS!
School Nurse
SICK JOKES
TONY: I GOT A GUPPY STUCK UP MY NOSE!
School Nurse: Here, blow your nose with this fish-ue!

YOU CAN EAT ***DIRT CHEAP*** AT THE ***SCHOOL CAFETERIA,*** BUT WHO WANTS TO ***EAT DIRT?***

MAD® ADD JOKE!

LETTUCE AND TOMATOES
+ PIG

SALAD BOAR

KNOCK-KNOCK?
... WHO'S THERE?
AL!
... AL WHO?
AL ASK THE **QUESTIONS** HERE SINCE I'M THE **TEACHER!**

TOM: I HAVE **MATH HOMEWORK** TONIGHT!

MOM: GO **FIGURE!**

COUNSELOR CRACK UPS!

LEN: WHEN I GROW UP I WANT TO OWN AN ICE-CREAM SHOP!

School Counselor:
You should go to sundae school!

ROSE: I JUST **SWALLOWED** MY **PICCOLO!**

MUSIC TEACHER: AREN'T YOU GLAD YOU DON'T **PLAY** THE **TUBA?**

WHY DID THE SCHOOL LIBRARIAN GET THE HEEBIE-GEEBIES?
... BECAUSE OF ALL THE BOOKWORMS!

GEOGRAPHY TEACHER: WHICH **CITY** IS ALWAYS **ANGRY?**

SMART ALECK: MAD-ISON!

MIKE: WHEN DO YOU HAVE TO TURN IN YOUR ***REPORT*** ON ***CONDENSATION?***

SCIENCE TEACHER: IN ***DEW*** TIME!

WHICH TYPE OF SNAKE IS ON THE FRONT OF A SCHOOL BUS?
... A WINDSHIELD VIPER!

GEOGRAPHY TEACHER: WHICH ***STATE*** IS ***MARTHA WASHINGTON'S*** FAVORITE?

SMART ALECK: GEORGE-A!

MAD® ADD JOKE!

PONY
+ SPIDER

HORSE N' BUGGY

WHICH KIND OF **BOOKS** DO **RACECAR DRIVERS** READ IN SCHOOL?

... **AUTO**-BIOGRAPHIES!

WHAT IS A HISTORY TEACHER'S FAVORITE FRUIT?
... DATES!

SCHOOL NURSE: WHY DO YOU KEEP **FLAPPING** YOUR **ARMS?**

JAYNE: TO KEEP THE **GORILLAS** AWAY!

SCHOOL NURSE: THERE ARE NO **GORILLAS!**

JAYNE: SEE? **IT'S WORKING!**

WHICH STATE SELLS THE MOST SCHOOL SUPPLIES?
... PENCIL-SYLVANIA!

WHAT DID THE BABY BIRDS DO BEFORE THE SCHOOL FOOTBALL GAME?
... THEY HAD A PEEP RALLY!

KNOCK-KNOCK?
... WHO'S THERE?
MARIAH!
... MARIAH WHO?
MARIAH IS HERE BUT I FORGOT MY LUNCH!

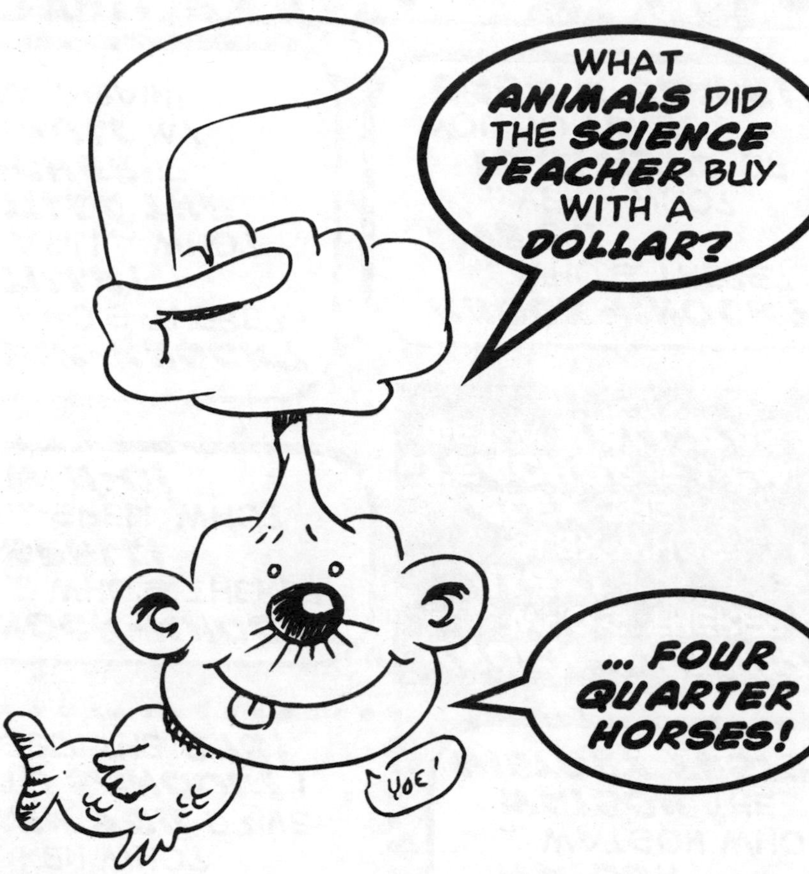

WHAT DID THE ***TEACHER*** SAY TO THE ***KITTEN*** WHEN IT WAS LEARNING TO ***SPEAK?***

... "PRACTICE MAKES ***PURR***-FECT!"

MAD® ADD JOKE!

GHOST
+ CANARY
BOO BIRD

KNOCK! KNOCK!

KNOCK-KNOCK?
... WHO'S THERE?
KEN!
... KEN WHO?
KEN YOU DRIVE ME TO **SCHOOL?** I MISSED THE **BUS!**

KNOCK-KNOCK?
... WHO'S THERE?
WATSON!
... WATSON WHO?
WATSON THE **HISTORY TEST?**

KNOCK-KNOCK?
... WHO'S THERE?
SPELL!
... SPELL WHO?
W-H-O!

KNOCK-KNOCK?
... WHO'S THERE?
ALEX!
... ALEX WHO?
ALEX THE **TEACHER** IF I CAN GET A **HALL PASS!**

KNOCK-KNOCK?
... WHO'S THERE?
ATILLA!
... ATILLA WHO?
ATILLA THE TEACHER IF YOU **PULL** MY **HAIR** AGAIN!

KNOCK-KNOCK?
... WHO'S THERE?
VERA!
... VERA WHO?
VERA RUDE OF YOU TO **TALK BACK** IN **CLASS!**

KNOCK-KNOCK?
... WHO'S THERE?
FRED!
... FRED WHO?
FRED I FAILED MY **TEST!**

KNOCK-KNOCK?
... WHO'S THERE?
SCOTT!
... SCOTT WHO?
SCOTT AN **"A" ON MY SCIENCE PROJECT!**

KNOCK-KNOCK?
... WHO'S THERE?
ORANGE JUICE!
... ORANGE JUICE WHO?
ORANGE JUICE GLAD I'M HOME FROM **SCHOOL?**

KNOCK-KNOCK?
... WHO'S THERE?
HARRY!
... HARRY WHO?
HARRY UP! THE **SCHOOL BUS** IS **COMING!**

KNOCK-KNOCK?
... WHO'S THERE?
WANDA!
... WANDA WHO?
WANDA GO TO THE **PROM** WITH **ME?**

KNOCK-KNOCK?
... WHO'S THERE?
BERN!
... BERN WHO?
BERN LUNCH? THE CAFETERIA **SMELLS!**

KNOCK-KNOCK?
... WHO'S THERE?
IVAN!
... IVAN WHO?
IVAN HISTORY TEST THIRD PERIOD!

KNOCK-KNOCK?
... WHO'S THERE?
SISSY!
... SISSY WHO?
SISSY RIGHT CLASSROOM?

WHICH ***STATE*** DID THE ***GEOGRAPHY TEACHER*** SAY YOU CAN ***WALK ON?***

... FLOOR-IDA!

WHAT DAY DID THE AUTOMOBILE FENDER VISIT SCHOOL?
... CAR REAR DAY!

HEALTH TEACHER: WHY SHOULD YOU ***DRY*** YOUR ***HANDS THOROUGHLY*** AFTER ***WASHING*** THEM?

DENNIS: SO WE DON'T GET ***RUSTY NAILS!***

MATH TEACHER: WHICH ***NUMBER*** IS THE ***MOST VICTORIOUS?***

SMART ALECK: ONE!

WHY DID THE JANITOR PUT UP A NOTICE IN THE TEACHER'S LOUNGE?
... HE WAS LOOKING FOR A BROOM-MATE!
YOE!

MUSIC TEACHER: WHERE IS YOUR ***FLUTE?***

CHERI: I THREW IT AWAY BECAUSE IT HAD ***HOLES*** IN IT!

MAD ADD JOKE!

DOG

\+ SPINACH-EATING SAILOR

PUP-EYE

WHICH STATE DID THE GEOGRAPHY TEACHER SAY TAKES THE MOST SHOWERS?
...WASH-INGTON!
DAD: HOW COULD YOU GET AN "F" ON YOUR SOLAR SYSTEM PROJECT?
LAD: I DIDN'T PLANET!
TEACHER: I HEAR YOU WENT CAMPING ON YOUR SUMMER VACATION. HOW WAS IT?
TIMMY: IT WAS IN TENTS!

WHAT DID THE ***STUDENTS SING*** WHEN THEY GOT THE ***ENGLISH TEACHER*** A ***PARROT*** FOR A ***PRESENT?***

... "HAPPY ***BIRDY*** TO YOU!"

IKE: WERE YOU ***INTRODUCED*** TO THE ***GIRL*** WHO'S THE ***PRESIDENT*** OF THE ***ASTRONOMY CLUB?***

MIKE: YES, IT WAS NICE TO ***METEOR!***

SPANISH TEACHER: SAY "**WATER**" IN **SPANISH.**

MIKEY: WATER IN **SPANISH.**

WHAT DID THE ***HOME EC TEACHER*** CALL THE ***PERCH*** IN HER ***PARAKEET'S CAGE?***

... BIRD-***SEAT!***

JAYNE: Will that hot dog be long?

LUNCH LADY: Yeah, about five inches!

JIMMY: I DON'T THINK I SHOULD GET AN "***F***" ON MY ***REPORT CARD!***

TEACHER: NEITHER DO I, BUT THAT'S THE ***LOWEST GRADE*** THERE IS!

TEACHER: CRAIG, DID YOU **DATE** YOUR **EXAM?**

CRAIG: I ASKED IT **OUT,** BUT IT WOULDN'T **GO** WITH **ME!**

WHY DID THE CIRCUS PERFORMER GET KICKED OUT OF CLASS?
... HE WAS CLOWNING AROUND!

KNOCK-KNOCK?
... WHO'S THERE?
OLIVE!
... OLIVE WHO?
OLIVE NEXT **DOOR, WANNA WALK** TO **SCHOOL** TOGETHER?

School Nurse SICK JOKES

PRINCIPAL: HOW IS THE GIRL WHO SWALLOWED THE SILVER DOLLAR?

School Nurse: No change yet!

JULIE: WHY DID YOU GET ***KICKED OUT*** OF ***DRIVER'S ED?***

JUNE: I HAVE POOR ***MOTOR SKILLS!***

WHICH STATE IS AN ART TEACHER'S FAVORITE?
... COLOR-ADO!

WHAT HAPPENED WHEN THE ***COMPUTER TEACHER'S DOG*** GOT ITS ***TAIL*** CAUGHT IN THE ***DOOR?***

... IT WON'T BE ***LONG*** NOW!

TIM: HOW DO YOU **SPELL "ISSISSIPPI"?**

TEACHER: DO YOU MEAN **"MISSISSIPPI"?**

TIM: NO. I ALREADY **WROTE** THE **LETTER M!**

WHICH **STATE** DID THE **GEOGRAPHY TEACHER** SAY HAS THE MOST **DIRTY LAUNDRY?**

... NEW **HAMPER**-SHIRE!

WHAT KIND OF SHOES DOES THE ENGLISH TEACHER'S PET WEAR?
... OPEN TOAD!
TEDDY: WE LEARNED HOW TO WRITE IN SCHOOL TODAY!
MOM: REALLY? WHAT DID YOU WRITE?
TEDDY: I DON'T KNOW, WE HAVEN'T LEARNED TO READ YET!
WHY DID THE TRACK STAR GO TO THE SCHOOL NURSE?
... HE WAS FEELING RUN DOWN!

TEACHER: MY NAME IS **ART** AND I'LL BE **TEACHING** YOUR **ART CLASS.**

STUDENT: MY NAME IS **DEE** AND I'LL BE GETTING **BAD GRADES** IN YOUR **ART CLASS!**

WHAT DID THE LUNCH LADY SAY WHEN HER KITTEN CLIMBED A TREE?
..."CATS-UP!"
YOE!

COUNSELOR CRACK UPS!

DIANE: I WANT TO BE AN ARCHAEOLOGIST WHEN I GROW UP!

School Counselor:
You'll dig it!

WHAT KIND OF ***PHOTO*** DID THE ***PHOTOGRAPHY TEACHER*** TAKE OF HIS ***PET TURTLE?***

... A ***SNAP***-SHOT!

GEOGRAPHY TEACHER: WHICH ***CITY*** HAS THE ***MOST EXECUTIVES?***

SMART ALECK: ***BOSS***-TON!

FRED: I'M GOING TO ***JOIN*** THE ***CHESS CLUB.*** IT MEETS AT ***KNIGHT!***

TEACHER: GIVE ME AN ***EXAMPLE*** OF AN ***INTERROGATIVE SENTENCE!***

CLIZIA: ME?

TEACHER: GOOD!

WHAT IS A *DOG'S* LEAST FAVORITE *SCHOOL SUBJECT?*
... MATHEMA-*TICKS!*
YOE!

MAD ADD JOKE!

BROTH
+ MUSICAL DRAMA

SOUP OPERA

PHIL: I'M THINKING OF TAKING ***DRIVER'S ED!***

LIL: THAT WOULD BE A ***GAS!***

WHICH STATE DID THE GEOGRAPHY TEACHER SAY HAS THE MOST TREES?
... OAK-LAHOMA!

KNOCK, KNOCK!
... WHO'S THERE?
RHEA!
... RHEA WHO?
RHEA CHAPTERS ***ONE*** THROUGH
NINE FOR ***HOMEWORK*** TONIGHT!

KNOCK-KNOCK!
KNOCK-KNOCK? ... WHO'S THERE? DAWN! ... DAWN WHO? DAWN TALK TO ME LIKE THAT. I'M YOUR TEACHER!
KNOCK-KNOCK? ... WHO'S THERE? DEWEY! ... DEWEY WHO? DEWEY HAVE ANY HOMEWORK TONIGHT?
KNOCK-KNOCK? ... WHO'S THERE? OMAR! ... OMAR WHO? OMAR GOODNESS, I'M LATE FOR CLASS!
KNOCK-KNOCK? ... WHO'S THERE? DREW! ... DREW WHO? DREW A PICTURE IN ART CLASS. WANT TO SEE IT?

KNOCK-KNOCK? ... WHO'S THERE? ROSE! ... ROSE WHO? ROSE BEEF IS WHAT'S FOR LUNCH!
KNOCK-KNOCK? ... WHO'S THERE? TAMARA! ... TAMARA WHO? TAMARA WE'LL BE HAVING A TEST!
KNOCK-KNOCK? ... WHO'S THERE? COLLIER! ... COLLIER WHO? COLLIER MOTHER IF YOU DON'T STOP ACTING UP IN CLASS!
KNOCK-KNOCK? ... WHO'S THERE? ESTHER! ... ESTHER WHO? ESTHER A WAY I CAN GET EXTRA CREDIT?
KNOCK-KNOCK? ... WHO'S THERE? ETTA! .. ETTA WHO? ETTA SOMETHING THAT DIDN'T AGREE WITH ME IN THE CAFETERIA!
KNOCK-KNOCK? ... WHO'S THERE? PATTY! ... PATTY WHO? PATTY MELT ON RYE IS TODAY'S SPECIAL!

SCIENCE TEACHER: WHICH **DINOSAUR** WAS THE **CHILLIEST?**

HUGO: THE **COLD-SAURUS!**

FREDDY: I GOT A **SPLINTER** IN MY **FINGER!**

SCHOOL NURSE: I TOLD YOU NOT TO **SCRATCH YOUR HEAD!**

JUNE: WHY DID YOU GET **KICKED OUT** OF **DRIVER'S ED?**

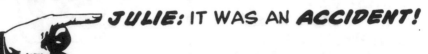

JULIE: IT WAS AN **ACCIDENT!**

WHY DID THE **GHOST** GO TO THE **SCHOOL NURSE?**

... BECAUSE HE HAD AN **EERIE** ACHE!

WHICH ***STATE*** DID THE ***GEOGRAPHY TEACHER*** SAY YOU CAN ***BAKE*** WITH?

... ***FLOUR***-IDA!

WHY DID THE TOILET GO TO THE SCHOOL NURSE?
... IT WAS FEELING FLUSHED!

MIKE: THE ***CHEMISTRY TEACHER*** HAS A ***DOG*** THAT CAN ***SAY*** ITS ***OWN NAME!***

IKE: YEAH, IT'S NAME IS "***WOOF***"!

MAD® ADD JOKE!

SODA
+ BIKE

POP-CYCLE!

TEACHER: I'M GOING TO TAKE MY **CLASS** TO THE **ZOO!**

PRINCIPAL: IF THE **ZOO** WANTS THEM, LET IT **COME** AND GET **THEM!**

WHY DID THE **CORN** GO TO THE **SCHOOL NURSE?**

... IT HAD AN **EAR**-ACHE!

COUNSELOR CRACK UPS!

PATTI: WHEN I GROW UP I WANT TO BE A SKYDIVER!

School Counselor:
That's bad, you're going to drop out!

WHY DID THE APPLE GO TO THE SCHOOL NURSE?
... BECAUSE IT FELT ROTTEN!
BIOLOGY TEACHER: WHAT DO SNAKES HAVE THAT NO OTHER REPTILES HAVE?
SALLY: BABY SNAKES!
DID YOU HEAR ABOUT THE CROSS-EYED TEACHER?
... SHE COULDN'T KEEP HER PUPILS STRAIGHT!

ENGLISH TEACHER: WHAT IS THE ***LONGEST WORD*** IN THE ***ENGLISH LANGUAGE?***

SMART ALECK: SMILES– THERE'S A ***MILE*** BETWEEN THE ***FIRST AND LAST LETTER!***

BARBARA: I'M NOT GOING TO ***SCHOOL*** TODAY, ***MOM. NONE*** OF THE ***KIDS LIKE*** ME.

MOM: YOU HAVE TO GO. ***YOU'RE*** THE ***TEACHER!***

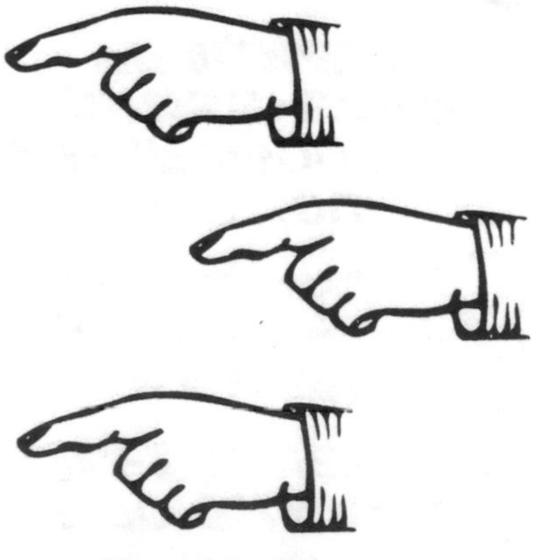

MAD® ADD JOKE!

RIDDLE
\+ CAR

A JOKES-WAGON!

BILL: I ATE ***TEN OMELETS*** AT ***LUNCH!***

GIL: THAT SOUNDS LIKE AN ***EGGS***-AGERATION!

WHAT KIND OF ***COOKIE*** DID THE ***LUNCH LADY BAKE*** FOR HER ***PET BIRD?***

... CHOCOLATE ***CHIRP!***

WHY DID THE **BABY BIRD** FAIL ITS TEST?

... IT WAS CAUGHT **PEEPING** AT ITS NEIGHBOR'S PAPER!

MIKE: I HEARD THEY SERVE **CRABS** IN THE **SCHOOL CAFETERIA!**

IKE: SURE, THEY'LL SERVE **ANYBODY!**

WHY DO LAMPS DO SO WELL IN SCHOOL?
... BECAUSE THEY'RE SO BRIGHT!
WHERE DO DINOSAURS GO ON THEIR SUMMER VACATION?
... TO THE DINO-SHORE!
JEFF: WHY DO BIRDS LIKE SCIENCE CLASS SO MUCH?
REBECCA: BECAUSE OF ALL THE BEAK-ERS!

NELLIE: I CAN'T REMEMBER ANYTHING!

School Nurse: How long has this been going on?

NELLIE: HOW LONG HAS WHAT BEEN GOING ON?

BILL: THE ***MATH TEACHER'S DOG*** HAS ***THREE LEGS!***

LIL: SO WHAT? ALL ***DOGS*** DO!

KNOCK-KNOCK?
... WHO'S THERE?
DARWIN!
... DARWIN WHO?
DARWINNING THE GAME 2-1!

KNOCK-KNOCK?
... WHO'S THERE?
ABBEY!
... ABBEY WHO?
ABBEY, C, D, E, F, G!

KNOCK-KNOCK?
... WHO'S THERE?
MARTIAN!
... MARTIAN WHO?
MARTIAN BANDS!

KNOCK-KNOCK?
... WHO'S THERE?
RITA!
... RITA WHO?
RITA GOOD BOOK LATELY?

KNOCK-KNOCK?
... WHO'S THERE?
PAT!
... PAT WHO?
PAT ME ON THE BACK! I JUST GOT AN "A" ON MY TEST!

MAD® ADD JOKE!

YOUR UNCLE'S WIFE
+ PIZZA TOPPING
AUNT-CHOVIES!

TEACHER: WHEN WAS **ROME BUILT?**

TOM: AT **NIGHT!**

TEACHER: WHY DO YOU **SAY THAT?**

TOM: BECAUSE IT WASN'T **BUILT** IN A **DAY!**

HISTORY TEACHER: WHICH ***PRESIDENT*** WAS ***GOOD*** AT ***SEWING?***

SMART ALECK: TAYLOR!

SCHOOL NURSE: JIMMY, STOP ***YELLING!*** I'M JUST ***LOOKING*** IN YOUR ***EAR!***

JIMMY: YEAH, BUT YOU'RE ***STEPPING*** ON MY ***TOES!***

RYAN: I'M THE ***TEACHER'S PET!***

MOM: THAT'S ***GREAT!***

RYAN: YEAH, BUT I CAN'T STAND ***EATING*** THE ***DOG FOOD!***

WHICH ***STATE*** DID THE ***GEOGRAPHY TEACHER*** SAY LOOKS MOST LIKE YOUR ***BEDROOM?***

... MESS-ACHUSETTS!

TEACHER: SPELL ***MOUSETRAP.***

ROB: C-A-T!

COUNSELOR CRACK UPS!

SCHOOL COUNSELOR: YOUR DAUGHTER THINKS SHE'S A CHICKEN!

Mom:
Don't change her, we need the eggs!

TEACHER'S PET

PART III

WHICH ***COSTS*** THE ***SPANISH TEACHER LESS*** TO FEED, HIS PET ***PARROT*** OR ***HIS SON?***

... ***TOUCAN*** LIVE CHEAPER THAN ***JUAN!***

WHICH ***PET*** DID THE ***GYM TEACHER*** TAKE ***CANOEING?***

... ***A WHITEWATER RABBIT!***

WHICH ***PET*** DOES THE ***LUNCH LADY*** HAVE?

... A ***POTATO CHIP***-MUNK!

FRED: THE ***ALGEBRA TEACHER'S DOG*** HAS ***TICKS!***

NED: THAT WOULD MAKE IT ***A WATCH DOG!***

WHY DID THE ***ART TEACHER*** CALL IN SICK AFTER ***HORSEBACK RIDING?***

... SHE GOT A REALLY ***BAD COLT!***

WHAT DO YOU ***GET*** IF YOU CROSS A ***CAT*** AND A ***DOLPHIN?***

... A ***PURR-POISE!***

WHY WAS THE ***GEOMETRY TEACHER*** MAD AT HER ***NEIGHBOR'S DOG?***

... HE HURT HER ***FELINES!***

WHAT DOES THE ***LUNCH LADY*** FEED HER ***KITTENS?***

... ***CAT***-ELOPE!

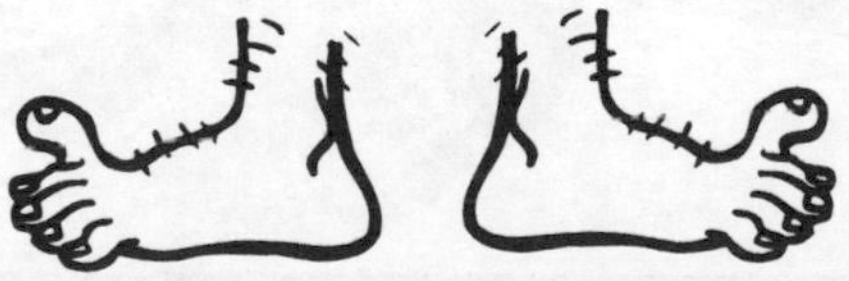

WHERE DOES THE ***SCHOOL NURSE*** TAKE HER ***PET FROG*** WHEN IT'S ***SICK?***

... TO THE ***HOP***-SPITAL!

HISTORY TEACHER: WHICH **PRESIDENT** WAS THE **CLEANEST?**

SMART ALECK: WASH-INGTON!

WHAT HAPPENED WHEN THE **JUMP ROPE** DID **WELL** IN **SCHOOL?**

... IT **SKIPPED** A GRADE!

WHAT DID THE **SCHOOL NURSE** GIVE THE **PIG** FOR ITS **SCRAPE?**

... **OINKMENT!**